Remembering What's Important

Priorities of School Leadership

Charles A. Bonnici

ROWMAN & LITTLEFIELD EDUCATION

A division of
ROWMAN & LITTLEFIELD PUBLISHERS, INC.
Lanham • New York • Toronto • Plymouth, UK

Published by Rowman & Littlefield Education
A division of Rowman & Littlefield Publishers, Inc.
A wholly owned subsidiary of The Rowman & Littlefield Publishing Group, Inc.
4501 Forbes Boulevard, Suite 200, Lanham, Maryland 20706
http://www.rowmaneducation.com

Estover Road, Plymouth PL6 7PY, United Kingdom

Copyright © 2011 by Charles A. Bonnici

All rights reserved. No part of this book may be reproduced in any form or by any electronic or mechanical means, including information storage and retrieval systems, without written permission from the publisher, except by a reviewer who may quote passages in a review.

British Library Cataloguing in Publication Information Available

Library of Congress Cataloging-in-Publication Data
Bonnici, Charles A., 1948–
  Remembering what's important : priorities of school leadership / Charles A. Bonnici.
    p. cm.
  Includes index.
  ISBN 978-1-61048-083-3 (cloth : alk. paper) — ISBN 978-1-61048-084-0 (pbk. : alk. paper) — ISBN 978-1-61048-085-7 (electronic)
  1. School principals. 2. Educational leadership. 3. Strategic planning. I. Title.
  LB2831.9.B665 2011
  371.2'012—dc22   2011012802

∞™ The paper used in this publication meets the minimum requirements of American National Standard for Information Sciences—Permanence of Paper for Printed Library Materials, ANSI/NISO Z39.48-1992.

Printed in the United States of America

To my colleagues and students at the High School of Fashion Industries, 1980–2002, and Louis D. Brandies High School, 1970–1980.

Contents

Foreword by Daryl Blank — vii

Preface — xi

Introduction — xiii

1 Surviving — 1

2 Improving Instruction: Guidelines for the Observation Process — 15

3 Improving Instruction: Alternative Observations and Other Practices — 33

4 Hiring New Staff — 41

5 Training and Retaining New Teachers: The Critical First Week — 57

6 Training and Retaining New Teachers: The Fall Semester — 69

7 Training and Retaining New Teachers: The Spring Semester — 91

8 Creating a Positive School Ambience: Respect, Instruction, Welcome — 107

9 Creating a Positive School Ambience: Support Services, Parental Involvement, Staff Development, and Punitive Measures — 119

10	Establishing Formal and Informal Systems for Creating a Positive School Ambience	133
11	Working with the Custodian and Physical Plant	147
12	Dealing with the Larger Context: The School District, Media, Advisory Boards, and Celebrities	159
13	Dealing with the Larger Context: Politics, Parents, and Panaceas	177
14	Passing the Baton	187
Acknowledgments		197
About the Author		199

Foreword

Like most school leaders, I am skeptical about another book on leadership. I picture another university academic preaching theories of school leadership without having been in the trenches of a school for any length of time. We have all been assigned such readings in graduate school and grudgingly fought through them. I am thrilled to be writing this foreword about a new book by Charles A. Bonnici. It describes battle-tested and successful best practices used during his 22 years as an assistant principal and principal.

How do I know these strategies work? I witnessed them firsthand. I grew up as an educator under the tutelage of principal Bonnici at the High School of Fashion Industries in New York City. Bonnici hired me as a social studies teacher; I participated in his new teacher workshops, experienced his observation methods, and attended the sessions he ran for aspiring school leaders. I am now proud to say that I am the principal of the High School of Fashion Industries.

In this book, Bonnici gives assistant principals and principals specific strategies to help teachers help students. At its heart is the expression of a core set of values making teaching and learning the top priorities. The systems Bonnici put into place are focused on helping teachers deliver quality instruction to their students. An examination of the chapter titles express Bonnici's values: "Improving Instruction," "Training and Retaining New Teachers," and "Creating a Positive School Ambience." These values were instilled at our school under his tenure as principal and continue to this day.

An appreciation of the educational leader's world is summed up in the title of chapter 1, "Survival." Here, Bonnici outlines immediate, resourceful ways to use funding and improve test scores. Bonnici explores strategies such as classroom assessments aligned to state exams and ways to identify students in need of assistance to help a newly assigned leader quickly gain momentum to make an impact on a school. He describes plans to avoid and handle staff missteps surrounding the improprieties of sex, money, and discrimination.

Primarily, the book focuses on specific strategies to improve instruction. Chapters 2 and 3 deal with the observation process, both traditional and alternative. As a "survivor" of Bonnici's observation methods, I can attest to how helpful his strategies are to the development of a teacher. The guidelines for his observation process value fairness and positive feedback to create a relationship of trust between teacher and supervisor.

Chapters 4 through 7 examine the hiring and retention of staff. The most valuable meetings I ever attended as a beginning teacher were Bonnici's workshops. We shared best teaching practices and learned to navigate the bureaucracy of the New York City Board of Education. Chapters 8 through 10 provide specific steps that an administrator can take to create and maintain a positive environment. Systems to create respect and a sense of welcoming are fully detailed.

Underrated responsibilities of school administration include effective dealings with the custodial staff, the media, and local politicians. Chapters 11, 12, and 13 outline how a principal can work positively with these and other entities to implement his vision for the school. Bonnici recognizes that effective use of these groups will support teaching and learning and that mismanagement will negatively impact the school's environment and even threaten the principal's survival.

From my perspective, one of the most impressive aspects of Bonnici's dedication to his students and staff was the way he left the school. He realized that all his work would amount to nothing if those systems he put in place did not live on after he retired. Chapter 14 is appropriately titled "Passing the Baton." I was one of those teachers that participated in a supervisory training program that Bonnici created for the next generation of school leaders at Fashion. I fondly remember sitting around the table in the principal's office while he shared his insights of supporting teachers, handling budgets and paperwork, communicating with parents, and thinking globally.

My view expanded from the 150 students I taught daily to a world where I could positively impact 1,700 students. These core values have stayed with me today as principal of the school. This book's power is in taking these values and transforming them into specific strategies to help school leaders help teachers help students. Fundamental to this book is the need for school leaders to always focus on supporting teachers and students. By reading this book, new or aspiring school leaders will learn how to take their own value systems and understanding of their schools' cultures to shape them into institutions where students can prosper.

Daryl Blank
Principal
High School of Fashion Industries, New York City

Preface

In my first book, *Creating a Successful Leadership Style: Principles of Personal Strategic Planning*, I describe how the persona created by the school leader can help him or her achieve success. This second book hones in on eight key areas school leaders must address to achieve this success during their careers, from their first year through their last. It shows the principles in action. Those who have read the previous book will be able to relate many of ideas presented here to what they read; those unfamiliar with that book will find that the strategies for addressing the key areas make sense in and of themselves.

I developed the content of this book while teaching leadership courses at Pace University, particularly the seminar for leadership interns. My graduate students requested sessions on specific areas they encountered during their internships. In a climate where school districts want immediate gratification, these candidates were concerned about the hostile climate that tends to greet newly assigned school leaders. They knew many newly assigned school leaders did not survive the first year. I provided survival strategies.

My students had also been confused by the different approaches to the observation process and wished to know how assistant principals and principals, teacher trainers and teacher evaluators perform this delicate task on a day-to-day basis.

These future school leaders knew theories about strategies for hiring the best teachers and they knew adult learning modalities for training them, but they wanted to know how real assistant principals and principals hire, train, and retain teachers. My response stressed the importance of the professional development given to teachers during their critical first year as educators.

They knew theories of management, but wanted to know how principals establish and maintain an orderly environment in their schools. I responded by providing strategies to create a positive school ambience. These graduate students had heard about issues revolving around the school custodian and asked me how a school leader addresses them. I helped them look beyond the custodian's office to the implications of the entire school plant. They raised many questions about the impact of the context outside of the school. I described my experiences with the district office, media, and business advisory boards. I indicated that school leaders have very little influence over politics, parents, and the yearly panaceas prescribed for schools.

I usually ended my seminar sessions by addressing a crucial topic that school leaders in training never think about: the passing of the baton; that is, the responsibility of school leaders to insure the continued success of their schools and its students after they leave due to retirement, advancement, or transfer.

In all cases, my responses were not hypothetical, but anecdotal, based on my own experiences as a teacher at Louis D. Brandies High School and then as an assistant principal and principal at the High School of Fashion Industries. The strategies described are those I used. Will they work for you and your school? Perhaps. This book provides you with a menu of ideas and strategies. As with any menu, you will select what you feel will work for your supervisory style and the culture of your school. You will also determine the priorities you will have for your school.

My entire experience has been in the New York City public school system, so my point of view is that of an educator in a large urban area with a diversity of populations. The strategies, examples, and anecdotes in this book come out of this experience. However, they are universal in application because a school, whatever its level or size or location, is still a school with the same goals and issues. A district office, whether in New York City or Tampa or Denver or San Diego, is still a district office, a bureaucracy.

Various schools, school leaders, and teachers appear in these pages. While their names are products of my imagination, they are based on the teachers, principals, and superintendents that I have known personally. All assistant principals and principals are in some way my alter egos. The incidents described and anecdotes related all actually happened.

Introduction

With the distractions of administrative paperwork, district demands, over-testing, and statistical mayhem, school leaders can forget that their main priority is the education of children. They can forget that their real clients are not politicians, community activists, media reporters or even central office personnel. Their clients are their children. A school leader's priority is to help these children grow academically, ethically, socially, and physically in a society with ever-increasing peer pressures and electronic wizardry.

New school leaders, whether principals, assistant principals or department chairs, face a myriad of conflicting needs and responsibilities. Which will best address the needs of children? Which will have the greatest impact on students? What should be addressed first? There are no simple answers. This book seeks to provide a menu of possibilities and strategies to help school leaders with this dilemma, from the beginnings of their careers to the end.

The first priority of a newly assigned school leader is surviving the first year. Chapter 1 provides strategies to help newly appointed assistant principals and principals keep their jobs, even if they are appointed to "schools in need of assistance." Once they survive, they can concentrate on the key elements of hiring, staff development, and school environment.

Student success is mainly determined by the instruction they receive. The vision, strategies, and plans of the school leader are meaningless if they are not carried out by the teachers. Chapters 2 through 7 deal with the hiring and training of the pedagogical staff. A school will not succeed if its leaders do not devote the majority of their time to staff development.

The staff and students work in an ambience that is at least partially created by the style and strategies of the school leader. Successful strategies are described in chapters 8, 9, and 10. Part of the ambience of a school is reliant on its physical plant under the management of a custodian. As described in chapter 11, this plant and its manager must also be part of a principal's ambience plan for the school. A school may have a positive ambience without good student achievement, but a school cannot have good student achievement without a positive ambience.

All schools exist in a larger context: the local community, the school district, the state, a myriad of local and federal laws and regulations, and the mores of society. The school leader will become more aware of these as each year passes. Once the priorities of instruction and ambience have been addressed, this larger context, discussed in chapters 12 and 13, becomes the next priority.

Finally, chapter 14 brings closure to the career of the school leader, providing a perspective on the final years of an assistant principal's or principal's tenure. It describes the reasons school leaders retire and the steps they take to insure their accomplishments will not be undone after they leave. Successful assistant principals and principals try to influence the future of their departments and schools by training the next generation and passing the baton of leadership.

Chapter One

Surviving

This book assumes that newly assigned school leaders have time to build relationships with their staffs and establish a positive learning ambience within their departments or schools. When this is the case, newly assigned school leaders still need to avoid pitfalls that could threaten their positions. This is especially true if they are assigned to schools other than their own.

When school leaders are assigned to euphemistically described "schools in trouble," they often find that the school district leadership or school board or superintendent or chancellor wants immediate results. Such principals or assistant principals have one year to turn the school or department around. There is nothing fancy about this job. It is simply one of surviving the first year. This chapter will look at both scenarios and provide strategies to help the new school leader make it through year one.

In the case of the failing school, before going forward, we need to take a step back to the application process of a prospective school leader. Candidates for leadership positions in troubled schools need to determine if they can make a difference. They need to check all available documents on the school and examine statistical data for the past several years. They need to read quality reviews and critically look at unofficial websites run by advocacy groups, parents, students, and the usual self-proclaimed local experts. They need to visit the school to speak with the current administration and the teachers they would be supervising. If a school is on a downward spiral and the school community as a whole is doing nothing to avert closure or reorganization, the candidate should withdraw from the pool of applicants. There is no glory in going down with the ship.

If, however, the candidate finds a critical mass of staff members and parents who want the students and school to succeed, then a change in leadership could make a difference. There are failing schools with dedicated teachers and concerned parents but inefficient, incompetent, and ineffective leaders. These ships can be set aright with new captains at the helm.

If you are appointed to a leadership position in a troubled school, the onus will be on you to effect an immediate turnaround. While you will want to concentrate on the priorities presented in this book, your first priority will be to keep your job and set the school on the road to statistical success. Let's be honest. This has little to do with improved teaching and learning. It is all about raising test scores.

Mike Juarez became assistant principal of grades three, four, and five in a southwestern K–5 elementary school. His predecessor, Sharon Slater, had been in the position for over twenty years and was "retired on the job" for the last three. During these three years, state curricula changed and promotional examinations in literacy and mathematics were added in grades three and five. Ms. Slater attended district professional development workshops, but did not turnkey the training for her teachers. Needed materials were not ordered. Grades four and five curricula were not revised to reflect state education department changes.

The principal, Ms. Willis, had been appointed two years previously. She was appalled by grade five test scores, far below the district and state average. Ms. Willis confronted her assistant principal. Ms. Slater assured her she would address this matter and then did nothing. She filed her papers for retirement before the principal could begin the removal process. Ms. Willis and her hiring committee of teachers and parents selected Mr. Juarez because they felt he was the most qualified candidate to turn around the upper grade department in one year.

Mr. Juarez looked at what could be done in grade five, as poor scores would mean students could be left back and not advance to middle school. He met with his six fifth-grade teachers. He provided a crash training program in the new curriculum and testing procedures. Together, he and the teachers analyzed the required exams and determined strategies students could use to improve their chances of succeeding. For one year, they turned the fifth grade into a year of crash learning and test preparation.

Fortunately, there was no problem with the third grade scores. His counterpart in K–2 had taken it upon herself to work with Ms. Slater's third grade teachers so that the three years of work done by her own teachers would be continued into the third grade when the children were given their first state exams. She even used part of her allocated book and supply money to buy necessary materials for the third grade. She and her second grade teachers met with the third grade teachers regularly to insure a seamless curriculum.

Mr. Juarez met with his fourth grade teachers separately and worked with them to revise their curriculum so students could build upon what they had learned previously and be ready for the instruction of the fifth grade. Ms. Willis was able to provide him with additional funding so that books and supplies could be ordered. The following year, when the fourth graders moved up, they would be ready for the regular fifth grade curriculum.

At the end of his first year, Mr. Juarez saw significant improvement in the grade five literacy and mathematics scores. They were middling when compared to statewide and district results, but far better than they had been. Some students had to go to summer school. A few were held back in grade five, but far fewer than in the past two years. These students had been taught what they needed to know to pass the state exams. They had learned appropriate test-taking techniques. Mr. Juarez preserved his position. The next year, with students entering the fifth grade having been taught the appropriate curriculum, the test preparation focus could be reduced in favor of real teaching and learning.

Test preparation for standardized exams can never be completely abandoned in today's world where success is measured by test results. All school leaders face the same challenge: to provide children with a good education while at the same time prepare them for the exams that determine their promotion and eventual graduation, exams that are also used to evaluate teachers, school leaders, and schools. These two goals are not mutually exclusive, as good teaching and learning prepare students for valid examinations.

There are some strategies that all school leaders can implement to help students meet promotional requirements and to improve test statistics:

- *Be sure the school is receiving its fair share of federal and state monies.* Most schools qualify for Title I and state supplemental funding to address the needs of below-proficient students. Some schools do not get all they are entitled to due to poor administrative procedures. Good administrators work with their parent associations to make sure that all students submit lunch applications to improve the odds of receiving significant federal funding. With new legislation pending, the criteria for receiving federal

funds might change; the school's procedures may need to be reviewed to be sure these monies are appropriated.
- *Identify students in need of assistance and analyze the district's statistical measures.*

School leaders should analyze how their schools use supplemental funds to insure the funds are targeted to the appropriate students. Idealistic new school leaders probably will not agree with the next few paragraphs, but acting on them could mean their survival.

The more sophisticated (not necessarily valid) statistical measures used by districts look at the annual growth of individual students and hone in on how well a school moves students from below-level proficiency to proficiency.

Mr. Juarez's district used a scale similar to that used in many school systems across the nation. Student proficiency on standardized exams was rated on a scale of 1 to 4 where 1 was "far below proficient"; 2 was "below proficient"; 3 was "proficient"; and 4 was "above proficient." The state's method for rating schools placed far more emphasis on moving "ones" and "twos" to "threes" than on moving "threes" to "fours." There were no gradations of "above proficient" and, therefore, schools had no incentive to set aside monies to enrich the instruction of these students.

Given limited supplemental funds, Mr. Juarez met with his fourth and fifth grade teachers and identified those students who were "twos" and "high ones" based on the grade three test scores from two years ago and the observations of fourth grade teachers from the previous year. He targeted all his funding at these students. He refined the focus to those needing assistance in literacy only, mathematics only or both. He refined further to differentiate instruction between native English speakers and English language learner (ELL) students. He provided targeted students with enrichment through after-school and Saturday tutorials. He made use of supplemental monies to reduce some class sizes.

This very efficient use of monies led to greatly improved test results—at the expense of almost totally ignoring the needs of those students who were low or moderate "ones" and all students already designated as proficient. This course of action was predetermined by the evaluation methods of the district. This was survival, not education. If Mr. Suarez did not make it to his second year, he would never be able to help any students.

For better or worse, with limited funding, school leaders need to analyze how the district will rate them and their schools. Using this analysis, they need to target funds to insure the greatest statistical increase possible. Having achieved the scores necessary to take their school off the "failing list" they can then re-deploy funds to insure a better education for all students.

This is cynical. It is also realistic. Today, we talk a great deal about improving the quality of teachers and school leaders to make our schools better. But behind this are two important realities: money and tests. The money allocated to education is never enough and cannot address the needs of all students. And, testing drives instruction. High stakes standardized examinations determine much of what is taught. States and districts better make very sure that their tests are valid and reliable.

- *Target students in need of assistance before they fail required examinations.* This applies more for middle and high school assistant principals and principals. The premise is simple: It is better to provide children with assistance *before* they sit for a high stakes exam to enhance their chance of passing on their first attempt. This was a mantra of Ms. Rivera in her suburban New York high school. Her assistant principals and teachers created placement exams in literacy and mathematics, basing them on the knowledge and skills needed on the standardized exams the students would face.

In June, incoming ninth year students were required to sit for these placement tests. Students were placed in regular classes, reduced size classes, and/or supplemental classes based on the placement exam results. In some areas, such as math and science, the students were placed on a one- or two-year track. Students were required to pass state exams in science and math usually given at the end of the ninth year. Based on the placement tests, students with severe deficiencies were placed in a course of study that allowed them to have two years of instruction before sitting for these exams, with the first year covering about one-third of the curriculum to allow for instruction in the basics these students just didn't know. Flexibility in the state exam program allowed for this variation.

Ms. Rivera knew that her placement exams could be wrong. She paralleled classes in English, math, and science for her ninth year. For the first three weeks, all classes followed the same curriculum. Teachers gave students additional placement-like exams and evaluated student writing and classroom performance. At the end of three weeks, adjustments in placements could be made on teacher recommendation with only minor disruption to student programs.

Over 80 percent of Ms. Rivera's students passed their required exams on the first attempt. With intensive assistance, over half of those who failed passed on the second attempt, bringing her overall passing rate to over 90 percent on all state required exams. What of the 10 percent who failed after two attempts? They were the students who would have been the low or moderate "ones" in elementary school. Almost all were failing classes in addition to failing exams. Some stayed a fifth or even sixth year, met their requirements, and graduated. Some later earned an equivalency diploma. Some never graduated.

By identifying and targeting students for assistance early, Ms. Rivera helped most of them avoid the loss of confidence that comes after failing an exam. She was also able to then give substantial help to the few who did fail.

- *Incorporate test-taking techniques into all levels of instruction.*
Require that all major teacher-made examinations use the same format as the required standardized tests. Have major class and homework assignments parallel the skills and tasks required by these examinations. Familiarity with the format and questioning style of exams raises scores. This is the method used by almost all private test-prep companies.

Schools should prepare their own uniform examinations to be administered at different points in the school year to simulate standardized testing conditions and insure all teachers are appropriately pacing their instruction. Such exams would also help identify students in need of help.

- *Analyze the questions and content of required state and district examinations.*
Standardized examinations emphasize certain skills and content knowledge over others simply because it is impossible for single tests of limited duration to test for everything in a grade level or subject area curriculum. Teachers can analyze past examinations to determine which skills and content to emphasize in their instruction, enhancing their students' chances of doing well on any exam.

The more content-oriented an exam, the better this strategy will work. A more skill-oriented exam is more difficult to analyze, but students can be trained to use standard templates and formats to address skill-oriented and essay questions. While she was in high school, Ms. Niles-Perry, principal of a large Los Angeles 7–12 school, was taught a method to answer all social studies essay questions—a method she successfully used (with variations) throughout her college career:

- All responses will be composed of five paragraphs: an introductory paragraph, three body paragraphs, and a short concluding paragraph.

- The first sentence of the introductory paragraph will reword the question into a statement. The next sentence will list the three major points that will be addressed in the body paragraphs.
- Each of the three body paragraphs will respond to the question with a major point, supported by at least three facts (names, dates, events).
- The short final paragraph will again restate the question as a statement and summarize the major points made in the body of the response.

Experienced teachers will be able to determine a template to teach students for any level or subject area, helping them deal with skill questions. This is a weakness of all standardized examinations: Good teachers and school leaders can determine the most important content students need to know and then can train students to use templates to address skills, improving their scores. Students so trained may have less knowledge and poorer skills than students not so prepared, but they will score better on standardized examinations.

- *Train teachers to use the rubrics to rate state- and district-mandated examinations.*

At the middle and high school level, mandated exams are often rated in-house. Assistant principals in charge of specific exams should not assume that teachers know how to rate these exams.

As much as school leaders try to insure consistency of instruction in all classes, every teacher is different. They each have their own variation on the standard and rate children differently. Teaching is an art, not a science. Children need to learn how to succeed when they move from one teacher to another. If they do, they will have a better chance of succeeding in college where there is far more idiosyncrasy of instruction, and in life where every boss has a different personality and expectations.

However, when we are rating standardized exams, such variation needs to be minimized. Ms. Valletta, now principal of a New York City school, remembers attending a state-conducted workshop for assistant principals. A new standardized examination was to be given that June and the state wanted to insure consistency of essay scoring. On the first round, these highly trained school leaders gave grades ranging from 50 percent to 90 percent on a sample essay. After internalizing the rubrics provided and practicing on more sample essays, the school leaders still showed a 10 percent variance in scoring on sample essays, which was considered acceptable by the state education department trainers.

While students were sitting for the state exam that June, Ms. Valletta duplicated the workshop for her teachers. She provided the rubrics and had her teachers use them to rate sample essays. There were some real donnybrooks during the training session, with some staff members complaining that the rubrics were much too difficult while others maintained they were so easy that the test was a sham.

Ms. Valletta neither agreed nor disagreed. She simply reiterated, over and over, that regardless of personal opinion, these were the rubrics determined by the state and, to be fair to all students, they had to be applied. There was still mumbling, but the variation of scoring on the samples decreased.

Ms. Valletta took other steps to ensure fairness and consistency of scoring. She divided her teachers into teams of two. She made this look random, but she paired those she knew to be hard markers with those she knew to be easy markers. All essays were read and rated by both teachers in each pair, and the average of the two grades was given to the essay part of the exam. As students took the exams by recitation class, she made sure that the exam envelopes given to each team did not include the exams of students in their classes. She made herself a team member.

She designated two of her most trusted staff members as re-readers. First, they reviewed all exam papers to check that the addition of the various parts of the exam had been done correctly. Second, they re-read the essays of all exams within five points of passing (in this case, all exams with a grade of 60 to 64). They were empowered to adjust essay scores. If, on re-reading, they felt the higher score given was the more correct score, they could designate this as the essay score. On the other hand, if they were more in agreement with the lower score, they made this the final score. If they struggled with the scoring, the paper was given to Ms. Valletta for a final grade determination.

No system is perfect. However, the above worked well for Ms. Valletta and her department. Every effort was made to score the exams fairly and consistently. In addition, there were two positive ancillary benefits. First, student and parent complaints about a grade usually evaporated once the rating process was explained. Second, as this process was repeated for every exam period, teachers internalized the rubric and unconsciously began using it in their classrooms and for their own and departmental exams.

The above strategies do not replace well-motivated instruction and well-planned lessons that address all aspects of the required curriculum. They are tweaks that help insure that students will be able to demonstrate their learning on promotional examinations. Mr. Suarez implemented many of these strategies; his department achieved the statistics needed.

The same basic strategies apply to principals appointed to schools in need of improvement. Such principals must work with the leadership team in the school, whether composed of assistant principals, chairs, lead teachers, master teachers, or coaches. The principal may present all or some of these strategies to create a plan for the immediate improvement of test scores and long-term improvement of teaching and learning. Those in charge of the different grade levels or subject areas will then implement, as Mr. Juarez did in the example cited.

Instruction is affected by poor school ambience. School leaders appointed to schools with poor ambience and discipline need to work with their security or safety teams, parents, and, in the case of older children, with the student government. Ad hoc committees must agree upon immediate, draconic, stop-gap methods to end chaos and allow instruction to take place. More monies from the budget may be devoted to deans and security personnel. There may be a short-term rise in suspensions and other interventions. Children may feel harassed.

In chaotic schools, new principals must compress the time frame and implement unrefined strategies immediately. Once the school is under control, they can iron out the details.

Survival can be an issue for school leaders assigned to successful schools with good statistics. In most cases, problems can be avoided if school leaders quickly learn the scope and legalities of their jobs.

Before he left for his well-earned retirement trip to Paris, Mr. Delderfield met at length with Ms. Valletta, the newly appointed principal of Manhattan High School. He took three huge spiral-bound notebooks off his bookcase and placed them on the desk in front of her. These books contained all the procedures, rules, and regulations of the district. Mr. Delderfield advised his successor to read everything carefully.

Today, such materials are available online in the "principals" section of a district's website. But, if anything, the scope of required knowledge has expanded since Mr. Delderfield's day.

It didn't take Ms. Valletta long to realize that her district's most critical regulations related to sex, money, or discrimination. This is probably true in every school district.

- *Sex.* Sexual misconduct can never be tolerated. A teacher can never have any type of affair, sexual or platonic, with a student. This seems simple, yet every day the newspapers have reports of teachers losing their jobs for sexual misconduct. In the movie *Moonstruck*, actress Olympia Dukakis puts this very simply in her conversation with the philandering college professor played by John Mahoney: *Don't shit where you eat.*

  Staff members also need to be discreet in their relations with their colleagues. It is easy to say there should be no office romances, but teachers are people and people can be drawn to one another. Where does flirting end and harassment begin? School leaders need to make all staff aware of how they should relate to each other; they need to immediately follow the prescribed procedures when there is an allegation of harassment.

  School leaders cannot tolerate student-to-student harassment. All staff must report any instances of such harassment; students must feel comfortable bringing such issues to counselors and the deans.

  Finally, liaisons between school leaders and the teachers they supervise are absolutely forbidden. If, for example, an assistant principal and a teacher find themselves drawn to one another, they need to make the principal aware of this immediately and request that one be transferred to another school.

- *Money.* Even in small schools, principals work with multimillion-dollar budgets. They must insure that if the budget shows a teacher has five classes, that teacher is indeed teaching five classes. If any staff member has release time for a special assignment, as dean, this must be duly noted in the budget.

  Careful records must be kept for teachers receiving extra payments for covering classes, coaching sports teams, supervising extra- and co-curricular activities, providing after-school tutoring, etc. There must be signed and verified time cards or time sheets. Any special programs providing payments to parents or students must be monitored in the same way.

  District procedures regarding school fundraisers and the collection of monies from students must be followed to the letter of the law. Likewise, staff must be made aware of the consequences of not following district regulations regarding conflicts of interest.

- *Discrimination.* This has a broad meaning in this context. School leaders must be unbiased in all decisions regarding staff members and must treat all staff members equally. Likewise, teachers must treat all students equally. Even the hint of favoritism must be avoided.

  In almost every school district in this country, corporal punishment of students is prohibited. Any allegation of corporal punishment must be reported and investigated as per the district's regulations. Some school districts, such as New York City, prohibit verbal as well as physical abuse. A teacher who disparages or embarrasses a student in front of the student's peers can face serious consequences.

  The teacher who in any way discriminates against a special needs student faces federal as well as district penalties. And, needless to say, discrimination of any kind between any members of the school community is forbidden.

Ms. Valletta learned quickly that it was her responsibility to make all staff—assistant principals, teachers, counselors, paraprofessionals, aides, custodial workers, security guards, and lunchroom workers—aware of these regulations. She had to report any untoward incidents to the appropriate district office. She had to investigate when directed. Any failure in any area could cost her her job.

While school leaders need to have an awareness of their district's regulations regarding the above areas, there are many other regulations that also need their attention. Principals have lost their jobs for everything from inappropriate rental of school facilities to failure to follow procedures to insure student safety on a school trip. The list is endless. Newly assigned school leaders need to spend their evenings reading the regulations. They also need to contact their more experienced colleagues when a question or problem arises and to consult with the person in the district office who can best advise and assist them.

School leaders may be appointed to higher positions in the same schools where they are serving or in different schools or districts. The location of assignment impacts on first-year survival.

There are advantages to moving up the leadership ladder in the same school. Such assistant principals and principals know the key players and culture of the school and its environs. They have established reputations among the members of the school community. They know what is working and what is not. New assistant principals will have the support of the teachers they supervise, their peers and the principal. It will be easier for them to survive, even if the school is in trouble.

Those appointed to a different school need to learn the culture of the school and the strengths and weaknesses of those they supervise. If the school is failing, there will be little time for finesse and they must make their staff aware that when a school is operating in emergency mode, some toes will be stepped on.

Even leaders appointed to successful schools walk a thin line between making an impact on teaching and learning and upsetting the existing apple cart. They do need to make an immediate impact in some small way to signal they will be dynamic leaders. This can usually be done through simple administrative improvements:

- Providing for better distribution and collection of books, equipment, and other materials.
- Using teacher input so that teachers are better satisfied with their programs.
- Posting their schedules on their doors so staff know where they are and when they will be in their offices.
- Using teacher input to order supplies needed by the department or school.
- Checking the bell schedule to be sure it best meets the needs of students and staff.
- Creating clearer responsibilities and lines of authority in the school.

Educational improvements are also possible:

- Making the observation and evaluation process transparent.
- Improving the training program for new teachers.
- Creating systems to improve the placement of students in the proper classes.
- Reducing interruptions of class time.

Only one move is needed to begin. Whatever change is made, reach out to the staff affected and seek their honest criticism. Make adjustments. Let it be clear that there will not be change for change's sake, but change that improves the ambience of the school for all. After consultation with the principal, assistant principals can then move their departments forward; after consultation with the district office, principals can lead their schools in new directions.

In successful schools, it is best not to make too many changes too soon. Sometimes, what is intended to improve a school or department has the opposite effect. A school's success gives new school leaders the time to truly understand the school community and bring about positive change incrementally.

School leaders assigned to a new location often make the mistake of referring to what worked better in their previous school. They need to remember that every school is different and what works in one may not work in another. No one wants to hear how it was done in the school leader's old school.

Once newly assigned school leaders have acclimated themselves to succeeding schools and implemented survival strategies in failing schools, they can move on to making a real impact on teaching and learning.

Chapter Two

Improving Instruction: Guidelines for the Observation Process

Hundreds of books have been written on the supervisory process, most espousing the best methods for helping teachers reach their potential. A major strategy is clinical observation, wherein the master teacher (the chair or assistant principal or principal) sits in on a class taught by a teacher and then meets with the teacher to analyze the lesson observed.

This chapter and the next are not going to provide any new theories on how this procedure should or should not be done nor are they going to attempt to provide a comprehensive framework on this topic. Instead, chapters 2 and 3 are going to provide strategies on how school leaders can make the observation process a constructive, positive learning experience for teachers. If this is done correctly, school leaders can reduce the anxiety of teachers being observed and the tension between their own seemingly contradictory roles of teacher trainer and teacher evaluator.

Many of the policies referred to below follow guidelines from the New York City school district, past and present. They are not unique to this district and most readers will find them similar to the policies and procedures found elsewhere.

In the past, a high school teacher had to be formally observed six times each year during his or her three-year probationary period. At least one of these observations had to be completed by the principal, the rest by the supervising assistant principal. Oddly enough, the observation requirement was less for middle and elementary teachers. Did they enter the system as better teachers and less in need of supervision?

Once a teacher earned tenure, the number of observations was reduced to two a year and then, after the teacher reached the maximum salary level (after eight years) to one observation a year. Of course, teachers in need of assistance could be observed more frequently. Today, schools in many urban areas are less centralized and observation polices differ from school to school. In general, less-frequent observation is detrimental to teaching and learning.

Lesson observation is the most important staff development tool an assistant principal or principal possesses. It is also a major forum wherein supervisors can permanently damage their relationships with staff members. The procedure for observations in most school districts includes a pre-observation conference which may or may not be lesson or teacher specific; a full-period observation or the equivalent; a post-observation conference; and a formal observation report which becomes part of the teacher's permanent file.

The following guidelines for the observation process provide strategies that will make this process effective and positive for those supervised.

1. *Never rate a teacher's lesson as unsatisfactory unless you plan to rate the teacher as unsatisfactory and seek his or her dismissal.*

This is a controversial guideline. In most school districts, a lesson is either "Satisfactory" or "Unsatisfactory." If the latter, the final report includes the reasons why the lesson was poor and a plan to help the teacher address each issue.

Schizophrenia surrounds the role of all supervisors of teachers, whether they are assistant principals, chairs, principals, or headmasters. Primarily, they are teacher trainers responsible for helping teachers achieve a competent level of instruction. At the same time, at the end of the year, they rate teachers based on their observations of their teaching, their evaluations of their other professional obligations, and, where applicable, their students' performance on standardized examinations.

Every teacher knows that no matter how supportive or friendly supervisors are in their role as teacher trainers, at the end of the year they become evaluators. So, even though the rating of the observation is the rating of a single lesson, it is the very rare teacher who does not see it as a rating of himself as a professional. And, it is the even rarer teacher who will maintain a cordial relationship with his supervisor after receiving a for-file Unsatisfactory lesson observation rating.

This guideline will reduce the supervisor's schizophrenia and emphasize the supervisor's role as teacher trainer. In essence it suggests that a supervisor never rate any lesson as unsatisfactory unless such a lesson is indicative of the teacher's overall performance and hence would lead to an Unsatisfactory rating and the eventual dismissal or discontinuance of the teacher.

Principal Thelen spent years as a supervisor in a large urban academic-vocational school. He only pursued an Unsatisfactory rating four times. In all four cases, it was his judgment that the teachers were ineffective in a variety of ways. Despite all the support he provided, there was no improvement in instruction. To him, these four teachers represented his failure as a staff developer and supervisor, for it was his job to make his staff competent.

In all four cases, he had no preconception that any of these professionals were incompetent. As each subsequent observation showed little or no improvement and as these teachers either took no advantage of supports offered (peer coaching, inter-visitations, and lesson-plan writing assistance) or showed no improvement in spite of taking advantage of them, he had to seek an Unsatisfactory rating. In the end, the task of the school leader is to insure competent instruction for students. If a teacher cannot provide this, the teacher does not belong in the classroom.

But, what should school leaders do when they observe competent staff members teach unsatisfactory lessons? They should give each teacher another chance. Even the best teachers can have bad days. School leaders remember that as teachers, they sometimes taught lessons that, for one reason or another, just flopped. Maybe they were not feeling well or had a poor night's sleep; maybe they were in the midst of some personal crisis. Or, maybe, the lesson plan just didn't work: They improperly assumed some prior knowledge; their timing was off; the motivation didn't engage the students.

Mr. Pfizer, principal of a Midwestern middle school, used to recount an anecdote from his days as a student teacher that illustrates such a failed lesson. In the 1970's, he was teaching mathematics in an inner-city middle school. Most of his students were African-American males from families at or below the poverty level. Motivating instruction was difficult. In order to teach his students about percentages, he hit upon a motivation involving the batting average of star baseball player and future Hall of Famer Henry "Hank" Aaron.

He thought this would be a terrific motivation. It failed miserably. Not one student in his class knew who Hank Aaron was. Sometimes teachers forget that students, for all their seemingly world-wise ways, live in confined neighborhoods and have limited knowledge or experiences outside these areas.

Ms. Valletta, principal of Manhattan High School, lived in Queens, an outer borough of New York City. In the 1990's, her daughter attended a local high school with a decidedly middle-class student body. Her daughter was stunned that many of her classmates had never used the subway to travel into Manhattan because they and their parents thought this marvel of modern rapid transit was unsafe. Constricted world-views are not confined to a particular class or area or city.

What strategies should supervisors use when they see a teacher's lesson fail? When the teacher comes into the office for the post-observation conference after teaching a poor lesson, the supervisor should immediately tell the teacher the lesson is not going to be written up. Once teachers know this, they will be more open in the ensuing discussion. If they are having issues with illness or a personal crisis, they can talk about this off the record. The supervisor's priority is always the competent instruction of students. But, as human beings, school leaders must also understand that sometimes the needs of self and family take priority over the needs of the school (or, as Captain Kirk says to Spock in *Star Trek IV*, sometimes the needs of the one come before the needs of the many).

The supervisor can have a discussion with the teacher as how best to balance both sets of needs. Does the teacher need a leave of absence? Is there anything that the supervisor or others in the school could do to help? (In some schools it is not unusual for the guidance staff to help teachers as well as students.) What reasonable time frame will the teacher provide for the return of instruction to its former level of competence?

A supervisor keeps in mind that not all teachers are equal. Teachers who have given long satisfactory service are owed more leeway than those who have just started teaching. Those who have freely given of their time and expertise outside the classroom are owed more consideration than those who are by-the-contract clock punchers. The supervisor juggles all these variables to best serve all involved.

Usually, the cause of a poor lesson is more mundane. It was just a bad lesson in that class, that day. The supervisor and teacher need to discuss what went wrong, what adjustments could have been made, and how to avoid the same problems in the future. Whatever the reason for the poor performance in this one lesson, the supervisor will inform the teacher that another observation will follow within the next few weeks. At that time, the supervisor will expect to see a satisfactory lesson. Competent teachers will fulfill this expectation.

New and experienced supervisors will approach the above method in different ways. Experienced supervisors have a history with the teachers they supervise. They have observed them many times. They have worked with them on multiple non-classroom professional chores, from curriculum development to test grading to parent conferences. Therefore, the observation process occurs within the context of their prior knowledge of each teacher, informing what they see in one lesson on one day. If they know the teacher has demonstrated competence in the classroom and other school venues in their history together, they know that a poor lesson is an aberration and treat it as such.

The new supervisor lacks this history and may be unaware as to whether a poor lesson is the exception or the norm. There are several ways a new supervisor can lessen the impact of this lack of knowledge.

- Newly assigned school leaders should make it a priority to meet one-on-one with each of the teachers they supervise. These should be informal meetings, designed to let each party get to know one another. The supervisor could ask questions that seek the input of each teacher: How do you think we could improve our curriculum? What do you think I need to know about this school (or department)? What advice would you give me? What questions would you like to ask me? The new supervisor will begin to form a professional picture of each staff member through this process and begin to have a "history."
- After the above meeting, the new supervisor should read the teacher's professional file. By reading observation reports, letters of commendation, and letters of reprimand, the new school leader will learn what prior supervisors thought about this teacher. However, the neophyte needs to keep two things in mind. First, and foremost, the assignment of a new supervisor to a school or department is a chance for everyone supervised to have a new start. Second, if there are negatives in the file, what evidence is there that prior supervisors provided the teacher with the appropriate staff support and development? Perhaps the fault for these negatives rests more with poor supervision than with the teacher's ability.
- New supervisors also need to speak with other supervisors in the school about their staffs. They should determine what their peers see as the reputation of their department as a whole and each teacher in particular. Even though these supervisors may never have directly observed the teachers in class, they have seen them around the school in their interactions with students, parents, and other staff members and may give the new assistant principal or principal important insights to add to each teacher's history.
- Finally, the new intermediate supervisor should speak with the principal. When Mr. Pfizer started as a chair at his Midwestern middle school, his principal gave him his thoughts on each of the teachers he would supervise. The principal had been in the building for over 30 years, so he had

a history for each. Every principal has preconceptions and biases, and a new supervisor must understand this. However, this is another source of information to help the new supervisor create a history for each teacher. Likewise, when a new principal comes into a school, he or she should seek out the principal who is leaving to learn the history of both the leadership staff and the teachers.

All this having been said, how do new supervisors respond to a lesson that is decidedly unsatisfactory? Even if they have done all the above and even if the history of the teacher indicates that the teacher is less than competent, the supervisor should give such a teacher the benefit of the doubt and not write up an initial Unsatisfactory observation report.

New supervisors who do this will earn their teachers' trust (see below), open the door to real staff development, and give all teachers a chance to prove themselves. If they observe the teacher in a few weeks and see yet another poor lesson, they should give the teacher the benefit of the doubt one more time and provide intensive assistance. If the third lesson observed is also poor, then the supervisor is probably looking at a teacher who will be rated Unsatisfactory. It is time to write an Unsatisfactory report and begin the process for the teacher's discontinuance.

There is one caution: Department chairs and assistant principals cannot operate on their own. Mr. Chen, principal of a Brooklyn high school, had a simple rule: No assistant principal will give a teacher an Unsatisfactory lesson rating without first consulting him. He wanted to review the facts of the lesson and check that the assistant principal was providing the teacher with all necessary assistance.

In most school districts, the assistant principal or chair may do most of the observations, but it is the principal who actually gives and must then defend an Unsatisfactory rating. An intermediate supervisor cannot seek a teacher's dismissal without the support of the principal or headmaster. Lacking this, the teacher will remain on staff. The supervisor will have to do all possible to remedy any deficiencies in instruction.

2. *Don't give in to the pressure to hastily judge new teachers as unsatisfactory.*

In most school districts, the process for rating a teacher as unsatisfactory is complex. Even the more streamlined process used by the New York City district today (a teacher may no longer grieve an Unsatisfactory observa-

A note on the New York City process: For many years, the removal of an unsatisfactory teacher for incompetent instruction required a legally defined process. First, the intermediate supervisor (assistant principal) documented incompetent instruction through the observation process; formal observation reports also documented all the suggestions for improvement and assistance given to the teacher.

The principal then observed the teacher and confirmed the judgment of the assistant principal. By March, the principal informed the superintendent of a pending Unsatisfactory rating. The superintendent or his representative came to the school to observe the teacher. Before this, all written documentation—the observation reports written by the assistant principal and principal and any other formal file letters—were reviewed. By reviewing all documents and then observing a class, the superintendent would determine if the judgment of the assistant principal and principal was correct and if the teacher had been given appropriate support. If this wasn't the case, the superintendent would not support the Unsatisfactory rating.

To remove an incompetent tenured teacher, this process would have to be completed for a minimum of two consecutive years. All documentation would then have to be reviewed by the district legal office at a Technical Assistance Conference before the chancellor's office would confirm support for the teacher's dismissal. This process was very burdensome, but it insured that every effort was made to treat the teacher fairly and that the teacher had been provided with the assistance needed to raise the level of instruction.

This short note leaves out a great deal about the process (e.g., at that time, a teacher, with the support of the union, could grieve every observation report—with each grievance requiring three levels of hearings—as well as grieve the final rating), but it provides a thumbnail sketch of what is called "due process" for the teacher, if not for the students subjected to incompetent instruction.

tion; he or she may add a written response to be affixed to the observation) requires that the negative rating be fully documented.

The pressure to rush to judgment is still present today as it was when Ms. Valletta first became an assistant principal nearly 30 years ago. At one of her first training sessions dealing with rating newly assigned teachers as unsatisfactory, she was told that it was important to judge a new teacher early. By the end of October, she should know whether the teacher was satisfactory or not. If the latter, she should begin the documentation process for a "U" rating.

She didn't accept this at face value. It was her responsibility to train new teachers, not to make a snap judgment to get rid of them. Then, as now, there were many alternatively certified teachers who had never been in front of a class prior to the day students reported in September. How much training could she give them in two months? She knew that the district was concerned about making sure that there was sufficient time for a negative rating to be upheld, but the probationary period was three years. At the time, there was a severe shortage of qualified candidates entering the teaching profession, so it was even more vital that she nurture those who showed some potential.

Ms. Valletta gave teachers time to develop and time to benefit from her training. In doing so, she risked keeping a less-than-competent teacher for a longer period of time; but, she was able to help most teachers become competent over time.

To be fair to the district, a few weeks later, Ms. Valletta attended another workshop that provided a different viewpoint. The workshop leader presented her and the other participants with a graph that measured a teacher's knowledge of subject matter and instructional effectiveness (see figure 2.1).

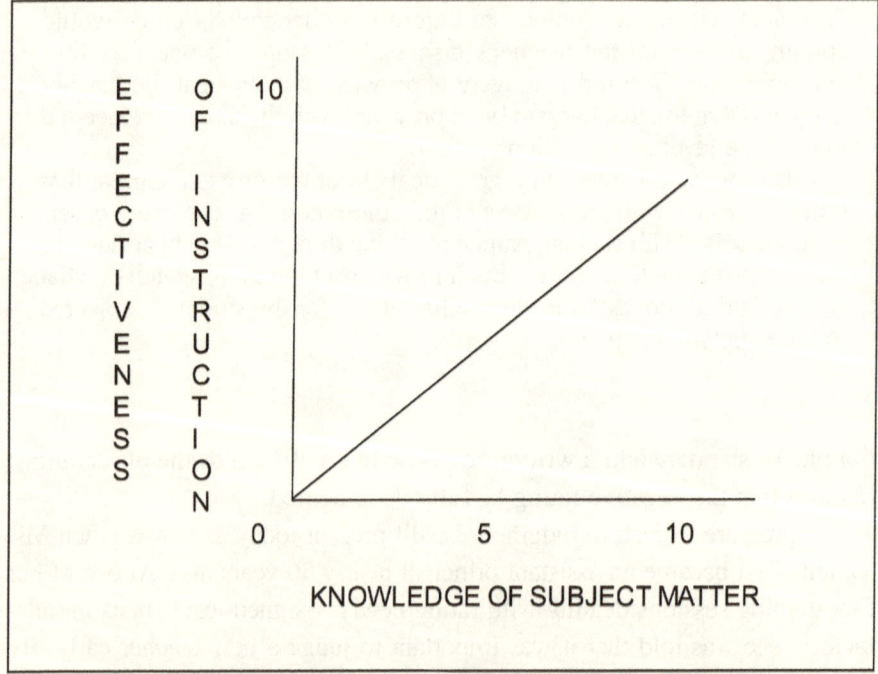

Figure 2.1. Teacher's Knowledge of Subject Matter and Instructional Effectiveness.

The participants were asked, "What is an acceptable level of instructional effectiveness and knowledge of subject matter for a new teacher?" Various answers were given, most between the range of three to six. The workshop leader then said that even if the proficiency was *zero* in one area and *one* in another, all of them had something to build on, for it was their job to train their new teachers. Of course this contradicted information given to Ms. Valletta in the rating workshop. In any bureaucracy, one learns to live with contradictions.

Once again, Ms. Valetta did not fully accept what was said, but she used this chart throughout her career as a school leader. She expected knowledge of subject matter from her new teachers. They all had an undergraduate or graduate degree. However, she did not expect much in the area of effectiveness of instruction, i.e., knowledge and implementation of appropriate instructional methodologies. She expected more of new teachers who previously had a semester of student teaching in a traditional university program than of those who followed an alternative route to certification.

When she became a principal, Ms. Valletta added a third dimension to this chart: a time frame for improvement. She asked herself, as both a teacher trainer and evaluator, how much time should she give a teacher to achieve a level of competence in both areas? Her answer varied by subject.

For a long time, there had been a surplus of English and social studies teachers. Therefore, her time frame for achieving a base level of competence in these areas was short. Conversely, there was and still is a dearth of special education, science, and mathematics teachers. Here her time frame was longer. As long as she saw continuous growth, she would retain a teacher rather than look for another and start from scratch. To do otherwise would be to have a revolving door in shortage areas and lose continuity of instruction.

How long should a supervisor give a new teacher to demonstrate competence? There is no one answer.

3. *It is important for the new supervisor to build trust in the observation process.*

A teacher earns supervisory certification and is appointed to a school as a new assistant principal or chair. One of his responsibilities is the supervision of a designated group of teachers. He begins to know them by building a "history" using different strategies. But, how will his teachers get to know him? Specifically, how will they learn to trust their new supervisor in the observation process so that he is seen as a support and trainer rather than as a rater "out to get them"?

Mr. Thelen thought a great deal about this issue when he first became the assistant principal of the English department at a large academic-vocational high school. He was younger than many of the teachers he supervised and inherited a department which had had little or no supervision for many years.

The observation format used by the district was composed of three parts. The first was a generic inclusion of standard items: name of teacher, date, class observed, period, class register, number of students in attendance, number of latecomers, and the topic of the lesson.

The second was a description of the lesson. This was to be an unbiased account of what occurred during the lesson. "Unbiased" meant it was not to include any judgmental words or phrases. For example, it would be inappropriate to state that during the motivation of the lesson "most of the students were inattentive." What does "most" mean? "Inattentive" is pejorative and therefore judgmental. Better and more precise phrasing would be

> Five students participated in the motivating discussion. One gave an extended response. Six students had their heads down on their desks. Two others were flipping through magazines. Three were talking loudly among themselves. Two were clipping their nails. One was eating a Big Mac.

It was important to be precise and unbiased because a teacher could only grieve a lesson observation on the basis that it was inaccurate or unfair. By making this part of the report precise, the supervisor avoided inaccuracies; by not using judgmental language, the supervisor avoided unfairness. Of course, this part of the report was written in such a way that another educator reading it would know immediately whether or not this lesson had been effective.

Mr. Thelen played with the format of the third part of the report. Most assistant principals used it to list "areas for commendation" and "areas for improvement." In other words, what was good about the lesson and what was poor about it. For the latter, suggestions for improvement were provided. Mr. Thelen didn't like this format because it was highly evaluative and directive in nature. It made the supervisor the active talker and the teacher the passive recipient of his wisdom. He didn't feel this led to real staff development. He changed the format and titled this part of his report "Major Topics Discussed at Our Conference."

Whatever the format, this third part of the report contained the supervisor's judgments and opinions. A licensed and certified assistant principal was entitled—and required—to rate a lesson. As long as this rating was based on the facts of the lesson (the descriptive second part of the report), it was considered fair.

Mr. Thelen used the following method to build trust in the observation process with staff who did not know him. After spending a full period observing a teacher, he wrote up the first two parts of the observation report: the standard information and the description of the lesson. When the teacher came in to meet with him, Mr. Thelen gave her a copy of these parts to read.

He then asked if everything included was accurate. In most cases, there was full agreement; in some, there was a minor disagreement ("You say that seven students were late; my records show only six"). Such discrepancies did not impact the report as a whole, so Mr. Thelen made the change. At this point, the teacher could relax because she agreed with her supervisor on the facts of the lesson. This allowed Mr. Thelen to begin the third part of the written report with the statement that "We agreed that the description of the lesson given above is accurate."

He then explained to the teacher that there would be nothing in the rest of the report that they did not discuss at the conference. When she left, she could be sure there would be no surprises in the written report. Even if Mr. Thelen later discovered that he forgot to bring up a topic, he kept his promise and did not include it in the formal file report (although in some cases he informally spoke to the teacher about it later).

Finally, Mr. Thelen made sure the final report was in the teacher's hands within two days of the conference so that everything they discussed would be fresh in the teacher's mind and she would not have to wait weeks to find out if he had kept his word (see item 6 below).

He used this method during his first year as an assistant principal. Once staff had trust in him, he no longer had to have the lesson description done before the conference, allowing him to schedule the conference sooner. He continued to use this method the first time he observed a teacher newly assigned to his department and for the four teachers who would eventually receive Unsatisfactory ratings.

Mr. Thelen became principal of the same school where he had served as an assistant principal, so his reputation as a fair lesson-observer had already been established. As he branched out and observed teachers who had not been in his department, he did not need to have the description done before the conference. Had he become a principal in a different school where he had no reputation, he would have gone back to this method.

4. *Let the teacher do most of the talking at the post-observation conference.*

This could also fall under item 3 on building trust, but it applies even after trust has been built. A supervisor will observe a teacher a few times a year. A typical high school teacher conducts approximately 900 classes a year (5 classes a day for 180 days). Even if a supervisor were to observe this teacher 5 times during the year, only .005 of the lessons taught would be seen. Therefore, a major goal of a supervisor's staff development through the observation process is to make each teacher a reflective practitioner the 895 times no one is observing the lesson.

Many supervisors spend the post-observation conference explaining to the teacher what was good and bad about the lesson. It is better to use this time to try to elicit this information from the teacher. A supervisor should try to view the post-observation conference as a lesson. A teacher's task is to elicit from the students rather than be the "sage on the stage." A teacher wants lessons to be student-centered rather than teacher-centered. Likewise, a supervisor wants the post-observation conference to be teacher-centered rather than supervisor-centered.

A supervisor should begin by asking the teacher, "What did you think of the lesson?" The above-average teacher will respond at length, usually giving an excellent critique of the lesson and describing what adjustments had to be made if there were any problems. Average teachers might need some follow-up prompts, as "If you were to teach this lesson again tomorrow, what would you leave the same and what would you change?" or, "If you were sitting in the back of the room observing this lesson, what would you say to yourself about what you had seen?" Such questions lead to more critical responses.

If major aspects of the lesson were omitted in the teacher's critique, the supervisor should ask even more specific questions: "I tallied very few extended responses during the lesson. Why do you think this was so?" or, "As students were engaged in the workshop part of the lesson, those in the groups nearest to me spent most of their time off-task. How do you think you could prevent this?" The supervisor should continue in this vein as long as the teacher provides appropriate and extended responses. When it comes time to write this section of the observation report, the supervisor will be able to include phrases such as

- You gave an excellent critique of your own lesson in which you . . .
- You felt that your lesson had gone well, but that it could have been improved by . . .

- We agreed that your lesson had gone well, but could have been improved by . . .

The supervisor quotes the teacher's own words. Once teachers grasp that they will be doing the talking at the post-observation conference, most will admit that this is a most difficult professional task. The goal of the supervisor is that teachers will end each day by asking themselves similar questions about their lessons, becoming reflective practitioners able to improve instruction even the 99.5 percent of the time they are not being observed.

Below average, barely competent and incompetent teachers have not yet been mentioned. In general, the strategies described above do not work with them. Ironically, the more incompetent teachers are, the more they think they are great. A supervisor attempting to elicit any type of critique usually will receive responses as

- The lesson was perfect as it was.
- No, I would not make any changes. It went exactly the way I wanted.

If the supervisor raises any specific issues, as that of few extended responses during the lesson, such a teacher becomes defensive, blaming the students—they did not do the homework, they didn't read the text, they are inattentive and lazy.

After much trial and error with such teachers, most supervisors find that the direct approach is best. The supervisor will do the talking, will describe what was wrong, and will explain what needs to be done to correct the problems. The supervisor will still incorporate the teacher's opinion into the written report: "You said that the lesson had gone well and that you would not have changed any aspect of it. I disagreed and . . ." A supervisor cannot develop introspection and reflection in those with little competence or sense of reality.

Finally, new teachers, particularly those who come through alternative certification programs lacking student teaching experience, need to be weaned into reflective practice. At first, the supervisor will be direct with them. Once they develop skills, the supervisor will lead them into reflective practice.

5. *Do not announce but do schedule observations.*
There were some occasions when Ms. Niles-Perry scheduled an observation in her Los Angeles 7–12 school. However, her general rule was to visit classes

unannounced. She wanted to see the type of instruction that occurred every day, not a specially prepared lesson designed for her. Her colleagues, who disagreed with this method, told her that if she saw the best a teacher could do, she could extrapolate to what the norm would be. Her response was "Why extrapolate when I can actually see a typical lesson?"

This may sound odd, but many of Ms. Niles-Perry's teachers told her they preferred the unannounced visit, comparing the observation process, even when they could trust their supervisor, to root canal surgery. Knowing a visit was coming and waiting for it was more nerve-wracking than the actual experience. Looking up and seeing the principal sitting in the back of the room unannounced jolted them for a few seconds, but eliminated all the time spent worrying about a preplanned visit.

How do unannounced observations build trust? Trust is in the teacher's knowledge that the supervisor will be fair in her judgments, not in whether or not the teacher knows in advance that an observation is forthcoming.

It is important for the supervisor to plan her schedule of observations to insure that she completes all the observations required in an appropriately spaced fashion. As a new middle school assistant principal, Ms. Hildebrand created an observation scheduling chart which she used each semester. When she became a principal, she shared her chart with her assistant principals and asked them to use it as a tool to create their own schedules (see figure 2.2).

Her assistant principals were asked to write in the names of the teachers they planned to observe, keeping in mind

- To schedule the *minimum* number of observations expected each semester: three for new teachers and probationers; one for tenured teachers.
- To take into account school holidays and dates of special school events (such as parent-teacher afternoons). These had a large X drawn through them.
- To schedule the first observation for new teachers within the first five class days; for probationers, within the first fifteen school days.
- Not to schedule any observations on Friday. Hold Friday as a make-up day for any planned observations that had to be cancelled during the week.
- Not to plan any observations during the last 10 class days in the semester. Again, these could be used for make-ups.
- To space all observations over the course of the semester and not clump them at the end.
- To plan a day or two for "department sweeps" (see p. 34).

WEEK	MONTH	MONDAY	TUESDAY	WEDNESDAY	THURSDAY	FRIDAY
1	SEPT					
2	SEPT					
3	SEPT					
4	SEPT					
5	OCT					
6	OCT					
7	OCT					

(continuing for the entire semester)

Figure 2.2. Supervisor's Schedule of Observations.

If, during this process, the assistant principal determined that any teacher needed additional observations, the observations could be penciled in—as could the observations required if it were determined that an Unsatisfactory rating would be sought. This flexible observation schedule would be part of the larger staff development plan for the department which Ms. Hildebrand expected from each assistant principal.

Ms. Hildebrand may have seemed a bit tyrannical about her insistence on using this type of scheduling tool, but she was trying to impress the importance of teacher development upon all her assistant principals. No matter what other responsibilities required their time, the training of their teachers was paramount. In addition, the completion of a required number of observations was used by the district as a criterion for the rating of supervisors. It was one of the few tangible criteria available.

Earlier it was mentioned that there are times when a supervisor will want to announce observations. Ms. Hildebrand did this as she trained her new teachers. As might be expected, her first visit indicated that most new teachers needed help with classroom management. During the post-observation conference with each new teacher, she provided strategies to improve management. She then scheduled an observation the next week, expressly designed to see how the teacher implemented these strategies.

Sometimes, Ms. Hildebrand taught a lesson for a new teacher to demonstrate a specific methodology. After she discussed the strategies she employed, she scheduled an observation to see the teacher implement the same strategies. Every now and then, a teacher invited this principal to a class to see a special type of lesson, often one featuring student presentations. She always tried to accept such invitations.

Ms. Niles-Perry announced all visits to incompetent teachers. In some cases, she reviewed the lesson plan with the teacher before the observation. She found that no matter how much support she provided or notice she gave for an observation, the lesson was still unsatisfactory. A borderline teacher can take a good lesson plan and teach a satisfactory lesson. An incompetent teacher can take a great plan which has worked well with every other teacher in the department and still not teach a competent lesson. That an observation was preplanned and announced and was still unsatisfactory only added to Ms. Niles-Perry's documentation for an Unsatisfactory rating. The teacher, despite assistance, was unable to execute the lesson and implement the pedagogical strategies discussed.

6. *Complete the observation process in a timely fashion.*

Tom Patrick is one Mr. Thelen's oldest friends. During Mr. Thelen's fourth year as a teacher, Tom was his student teacher. Later, Tom was a teacher in Mr. Thelen's department and, for a short time, an assistant principal after Mr. Thelen became principal. (Tom relocated to continue as an educator in the suburbs.) Tom kindly referred to Mr. Thelen as "the Assassin" because of the time frame of his observation process. Mr. Thelen tried to complete the process in one day. He would observe a teacher early in the day, have the post-observation conference in the middle of the day, and have the observation report in the teacher's mailbox before the school day ended. The one-day process was always his goal, one not always attained;

but Mr. Thelen always made sure the entire process was completed within three days.

The observation process is a major component of staff development. Holding the post-observation conference as soon as possible after the observation ensures that the lesson is fresh in the mind of both the teacher and the observer. Providing feedback on the observation and conference reduces the teacher's anxiety about what the report will contain. It allows the teacher to implement agreed-upon suggestions for improvement so that there is an immediate, positive impact on instruction. The longer the time frame between the observation and the conference and between the conference and the report, the less effective the process is.

Everyone reading this chapter has experienced the exact opposite: You were observed and the post-observation conference was not held for several weeks. You did not receive the formal report until the change of seasons. Assistant principals and principals are busy. No matter how well they plan their time, there are multiple interruptions. They can point to a myriad of legitimate excuses for such delays. But, if the improvement of instruction is the main priority of the school leader, none of these excuses is acceptable. Completion of the observation process in a timely fashion to maximize impact upon instruction is the main priority. If it is treated as such, it will get done.

So, was Tom right? Was Mr. Thelen an "assassin" in his approach to this process? If by that word Tom meant that Mr. Thelen acted quickly and decisively to improve instruction, then yes. In the end, every reflective practitioner appreciates receiving feedback in a timely fashion, just as every student wants to get his test back the next day.

These six guidelines are open to adaptation to the norms of different schools and districts. However, their implementation will make the process more meaningful for staff and lead to improved instruction for students. Additional suggestions for the observation process follow in the next chapter.

Chapter Three

Improving Instruction: Alternative Observations and Other Practices

In attempting to implement the six guideless for the observation process described in chapter 2, school leaders need to consider many related matters, from making use of alternative methods of observation to the inherent difficulty of critiquing a teacher who is also a personal friend. These and other musings on the process are the subject of this chapter.

All the strategies described in chapter 2 relate to formal full-period observations. There are many other types of observation that should be a part of a supervisor's repertoire.

- On the first day of classes, assistant principals or chairs should informally observe all the new teachers in their departments or grade levels during the first 10–15 minutes of a lesson. When they become principals, they should do likewise with all new teachers in the school. At the end of the period, they should stop by again to go over with the teacher any issues they may have seen. They should follow up with a short, informal letter placed in each teacher's mailbox by the end of the day.

  Of course, prior to the first day of instruction, these supervisors have met with their new staff and reviewed what to do on the first day and during the first week (see chapter 5). They have informed their teachers to expect such a short visit to see if they are implementing what has been discussed. The supervisors also want to make sure that their neophytes aren't doing anything that will cost them control of their classes for the rest of the semester. Finally, these assistant principals and principals are sending the message that good instruction is the highest priority of the school.

- A similar procedure can be used during the semester. For example, a supervisor might observe all the social studies teachers of seventh grade classes for 10–15 minutes on the same day. The supervisor can determine if the teachers are following the calendar of the syllabus and can evaluate the consistency of instruction. The supervisor then sends each teacher a short, informal letter within the next day or two. This procedure works extremely well in math, science, foreign language, and social studies where teachers of the same course on the same level should more or less be at the same place in the curriculum. If this is not the case, then corrections are needed.
- A principal can add two variations on this procedure. In one, the principal schedules a "department sweep" with each assistant principal. On this day, they make 10–15 minute visits to each teacher supervised by the assistant principal. In addition to getting a feel for instruction in this department on this day, the principal will also be able to gauge if the department supervisor knows the strengths and weaknesses of the teachers in the department. Before going into each class, the principal will ask the department supervisor what they should expect to see. After leaving, the principal will ask for an analysis of what was observed and, if appropriate, what type of support is being provided to the teacher.
- In the other variation, a principal selects a student at random and follows his program for the day, observing each of this student's teachers for about 10 minutes. There is no better way to see what students are experiencing during their school day. The principal will send the teachers observed a short, informal, positive letter. If any problems are seen, the principal will have the appropriate supervisor follow up with the teacher.
- Sometimes teachers need improvement in one aspect of instruction. Ms. Rivera, in her suburban high school, found that teachers often had time management issues at the beginning or end of a lesson. If she saw a teacher had problems beginning a lesson, she arranged to observe the teacher during the first 10 minutes of four lessons over the next two weeks to see if he or she were implementing the strategies they discussed on the most effective ways to begin a lesson. After the last of these observations, she would have a post-observation conference; the four 10-minute observations would be combined in one report.
- Many supervisors offer teachers a digital recording option. A teacher agreeing to this procedure would arrange to have a lesson recorded. The teacher would view the recording and have the option of ending the pro-

cess at this point. If the teacher decided to continue, the teacher and the supervisor would look at the recording together and have the usual post-observation conference. During her many years as a Houston elementary school principal, Ms. Nguyen had only one teacher agree to this method. In our increasingly technological world, newer teachers may be more comfortable with this option. However, seeing themselves, no matter how good they are, might be too intense for many teachers.
- Finally, as school leaders walk about their schools on their daily strolls, they look into classrooms and if anything seems interesting (or amiss), they stop in for a few minutes. As they leave, they thank the teacher. They are stressing the priority of instruction.

Above, reference is made to short informal letters to teachers as opposed to formal observation reports. In many districts, there are contractual distinctions between the two. A non-file, or informal, letter is just that, a letter to the teacher with no copy in the teacher's official file. A formal observation or letter is placed in the file. It includes a signature line where the teacher acknowledges receipt of the letter and its placement in his or her professional file.

However, in the Kafkaesque world of school districts, non-file letters may become part of the formal file within a specified period of time. Ms. Niles-Perry saw chaos in the classroom of a borderline teacher. She sent him an informal letter with pointers on classroom management. She also spoke to the teacher's immediate supervisor and directed him to provide additional support. A month later, Ms. Niles-Perry formally observed the teacher and again saw chaos. In her formal observation report, she referred to the suggestions she had made in the informal letter from the previous month and affixed a copy, making the informal letter part of the formal file. She also described the support provided by the immediate supervisor.

Intermediate supervisors who act in the place of their principals need to be cautious in implementing the ideas of this and the previous chapter. If intermediate supervisors go to their principals enthusiastic about the guidelines for the observation process and alternative forms of observation and their principals reject them and provide their own guidelines, they must do what their principals want. Of course, the assistant principals or chairs can try to convince their principals of the efficacy of these strategies, but in the end, their principals set the rules.

If a principal says that the conference notes should consist of pluses and minuses, the supervisor will give pluses or minuses. If the principal wants a checklist to be used for observations, the supervisor will use a checklist. The intermediate supervisor carries out the policies of the principal—and is rated by the principal.

There are other practical strategies relating to the observation process that the principal or assistant principal should consider. This chapter would be incomplete without the following bits of advice.

What should a school leader do while observing a class? Ms. Nguyen remembers her principal falling asleep in the back of her room and snoring loudly. Ms. Hildebrand remembers her department supervisor doing crossword puzzles. Conversely, Ms. Niles-Perry remembers her principal frowning throughout the lesson while writing furiously. Mr. Pfizer remembers his department supervisor joining in the lesson as a student. Mr. Chen had a supervisor who brought her laptop and word processed the report as she was watching him teach. All school leaders have heard stories about principals and assistant principals interrupting lessons while observing or correcting a teacher's mistakes or even taking over the class.

As an assistant principal and principal, Mr. Pfizer had personal guidelines for himself as a visitor and observer:

- He arrived at the classroom before most students arrived. He greeted the teacher. His teachers knew all his observations were unannounced, but if a teacher told Mr. Pfizer that she felt ill that day or that class was a full-period examination, he would usually postpone the observation and go to a back-up plan for that period. Of course, he did sometimes observe examinations and provide teachers with suggestions on creating and proctoring tests. And, if a teacher always pleaded illness he would schedule a meeting to discuss this matter.
- After greeting the teacher, he stood at the rear of the room until the students entered and took their seats. He then took a vacant seat near the back of the room.
- During the lesson, he stayed attentive and smiled at the appropriate times. He took notes on the lesson, but did not write continuously. He was looking at the students' reaction to the instruction and the manner of the teacher.
- Sometimes, a teacher called on him as if he were a class member. If a teacher took this tack, Mr. Pfizer played the role accordingly.

- Except as indicated above, he would not interrupt or interfere with the lesson, but play the part of a fly on the wall. If the teacher made an egregious error, he said nothing in front of the students. If the opportunity presented itself, he quietly spoke to the teacher during the class so she could correct the error. Otherwise, he spoke to her after the class so she could correct the matter the next day.
- Even if the class were unruly or unresponsive, he would not interfere or take over the class himself. To do so would totally undercut the teacher's credibility with the class. He would work with the teacher during the post-observation conference to correct these problems. In his mind, there would be one exception to this guideline: If he saw that a child or the teacher were in danger of physical harm, he would intervene. This never happened.
- During the lesson, he would unobtrusively ask to see the notebooks of several of the students near where he was sitting.
- At the end of the lesson, he would thank the teacher for welcoming him to the class and set up the post-observation conference.

School leaders would do well to emulate Mr. Pfizer's courtesy and unobtrusive guidelines, as they show respect for the professionalism of the teacher, support the teacher's authority in the class, and allow instruction to proceed normally.

Mr. Thelen, principal of an academic-vocational school, had a variation on these guidelines when observing shop classes where the teacher circulated, providing one-on-one instruction as students worked on individual or group projects. After several observations, he felt that there should be whole class interaction at the beginning of each period. He discussed this with the assistant principal of occupational subjects and she agreed to initiate a new procedure with her teachers: They would begin each shop class with a mini-lesson in which they brought the students together and elicited a description of what the class was working on.

This mini-lesson helped Mr. Thelen understand what the students were doing. Then he circulated and spoke to students individually, asking them to explain to him what they were doing. The better the explanation of the student, the better the instruction that had been given.

School leaders should avoid getting too friendly with the teachers they supervise. We are all human. We like some people we work with more than others. We discover that some of our staff share the same interests we have.

But, getting too friendly with staff members leaves a supervisor open to the perception of favoritism even if none exists. In addition, any friendships supervisors foster may be tested when they need to tell staff members that they taught a poor lesson. It is a rare friendship that can weather direct criticism.

Over time, Ms. Nguyen developed friendships with some of her veteran teachers. She and her husband would plan activities with them and their significant others. However, she made it clear that her responsibility to the students of the school came before her friendship with them. There never was an instance where the two came into conflict.

Not developing friendships does not mean one should not be friendly. This type of friendly connection may manifest itself in post-observation conferences. Ms. Rivera, principal of a large high school in suburban New York, frequently brings up a book or article she read relevant to the topic of the lesson she just observed. Often, this leads to a sharing of recent reading. She and her social studies teachers often loan each other books. She and two other teachers sometimes exchange the latest mystery or science fiction books each reads. Such seemingly tangential types of conversation are sometimes just as important as the direct analysis of the lesson itself for they put the lesson in the context of the teacher's professional and personal reading and experiences. Teachers want to see their school leaders not only as teacher trainers and managers, but as scholars in their fields and generalists in their personal reading.

In today's world, there seems to be a youth movement for school leaders. It is not unusual for a principal to be in his late twenties or early thirties. Age is not an issue, experience is. In chapter 2 it was noted that when Mr. Thelen began as a supervisor, he was younger than most of the teachers in his department. However, he had over nine years of teaching experience. When he spoke about pedagogy, he knew what he was talking about. Today, many youthful principals may have less than three years of teaching experience. Experienced teachers will question their professional credentials. The principal is, to use the British term, the "headmaster" or what we would call the "master teacher." It takes time to gain this status and today we have too many principals who may know theory and have managerial backgrounds, but who are not master teachers.

After intermediate supervisors hone their observation and leadership skills, many will aspire to become principals. One of the first questions they may ask themselves is how they will observe and supervise teachers outside their areas of expertise. Upon becoming principal of a middle school, Mr. Pfizer, a former math teacher, had to observe teachers of social studies, science, English, foreign language, wood shop, art, music, and physical education. Some aspects of teaching are the same across disciplines. These he knew. For the others, he spoke with the subject-area supervisors and master teachers to learn about the unique aspects of instruction in these areas.

For example, after he observed a Spanish lesson he was unsure of some aspects of lesson organization and methodology in languages other than English. Before he scheduled the post-observation conference, he spoke with the lead foreign language teacher, discussed what he observed, and had his questions answered. After several years, he had learned a great deal about instruction in all subject areas and felt more competent in his judgments.

A single observation is but the merest sliver of what a teacher does during the course of a year. How can supervisors expand their knowledge of the quality of instruction without increasing the number of formal observations? Several methods were discussed above: informal observations, short stop-ins, and conversations with teachers. Another way to maximize the knowledge gained from the formal observation is to incorporate the examination of student notebooks.

While the lesson is but one of hundreds in the year, student notebooks will tell the supervisor all that went before the lesson, the quality of the teacher's board work as reflected in the students' notes, the types of assignments given, the quality of teacher feedback, and the appropriateness of the examinations given. While an assistant principal, Ms. Hildebrand would note which students provided the most appropriate responses during the first half of a lesson she was observing. When the opportunity presented itself, she would unobtrusively ask these students, most likely the better students in the class, if she could borrow their notebooks for a few minutes. Sometimes, she checked the grades of the students in the class before visiting so that she could review the notebooks of those students with the highest grades.

Many observation methods stress watching what the teacher does. Savvy supervisors learn much more by observing what the students do. In their observation reports, they make reference to what the students were doing at various times during the lesson. For example:

> During the discussion of the results of the Treaty of Versailles, I observed that 10 students gave extended responses. Every student I looked at was attentive

and taking notes. Two students said that they did not understand some point so you had other students explain these points again.

In a case like this, it is obvious that the teacher had engaged the class and was using excellent pedagogical techniques. A supervisor will learn more about the effectiveness of the instruction in any class by observing the students more than the teacher.

The observation process is part of the professional development program and evaluation process in every school district. A supervisor can lessen the schizophrenia of these two purposes by implementing constructive strategies to earn the trust of teachers and improve the instruction teachers provide their students.

Chapter Four

Hiring New Staff

This chapter has a before and after feel to it, reflecting changes in hiring practices over the past several years. For a long time, a principal's control over hiring was limited by contractual provisions on seniority transfer and the need of the district to place teachers excessed from schools with decreasing enrollments. Up until the last few years, savvy principals had to work their way around these limitations to gain some control over the hiring process. Even the wiliest were sometimes forced to take on teachers they did not want. Unfortunately, some school systems are still in this Byzantine state. The first part of this chapter will concern itself with manipulating a system designed to take the task of hiring away from principals.

As school districts make school leaders more accountable, it becomes difficult for them to deny principals the authority to hire their own staffs. The New York City (NYC) school district is an example. Several years ago, the district negotiated a new contract that eliminated the seniority transfer process. At the same time, the district established "teacher pools" of excessed teachers so the teachers were not sent to schools unless a principal requested them. The principals of the city, who always complained about their lack of control over the hiring process, should have celebrated. The second part of this chapter addresses systems where principals have control over hiring. It could be subtitled "Be Careful What You Wish For."

Let's look at how this first scenario worked in the NYC school district, representative of many urban, suburban, and even rural districts. Principals projected their needs for the coming September in the spring of the previous year. This projection could be adjusted in the fall based on new or unexpected circumstances. Variables such as projected student enrollment, teacher leaves, sabbaticals, and retirements were used to estimate the number of teaching vacancies for the upcoming school year. On the middle and high school level, this projection was refined to indicate the subject areas of the vacancies.

The district reviewed the information submitted by the principal and sent each a summary of the expected vacancies. The district asked each principal to indicate which vacancies were to be posted on the union transfer list. By contract, half of the projected vacancies had to be listed. Teachers with more than a certain number of years experience could apply for these vacancies. If more than one applied for the same vacancy, it was awarded to the teacher with the most district-wide seniority. Sometimes, no one applied for a certain vacancy, so the position reverted back to the principal's prerogative. More often there was an applicant, and in September a teacher the principal had never even interviewed showed up at the school to take a position. This was only the beginning of the staffing problems.

It is late August or early September. The principal has been informed how many vacancies will be filled by transfer—maybe. Sometimes, this information actually came to the principal after the transfers showed up on the first day of school in September. Sometimes, the principal was told to expect a transfer who then changed his or her mind and decided to stay in his or her school. For the moment, let's not deal with this bureaucratic catch-22.

Typically, principals started going through resumes in April and interviewing prospective candidates for the vacancies that were theirs to fill. These candidates were mainly spring graduates from traditional university and alternative certification programs. Principals also went to district-sponsored job fairs to find additional candidates. Since they had a projected and not a final budget, they were never 100 percent sure that any position would actually exist, so they could only make tentative job commitments. Affluent suburbs often had their budgets fixed before the summer and could give definite commitments, contracts, and higher salaries to their applicants.

This budget issue may sound strange, but in a large bureaucracy it is usually the norm. School budgets in NYC are based on a variety of factors, the most important of which is the New York Stock Exchange. City coffers are flush when the market does well. Profits are taxed as are the bloated bonuses given to corporate executives. Another factor is the New York State contribution to the city, often not settled until October when the state legislature and governor finally agree on a budget.

The federal government also provides Title I funds based on student need and poverty level. In good times, all of these funding sources coalesce so that a school receives close to what the district number crunchers consider "full funding." When there are shortfalls, this "full funding" budget is reduced by 5 percent, 10 percent, or even more in the severe budget crises that periodically occur.

When budgets are projected in mid-spring for the following fall, it is rarely known what percentage of full funding will actually be available. And that's not the worst of it. In mid-spring, the principals had to project their student enrollment as of October 31 of the fall semester. Their budget allocations were dependent on this enrollment projection. Principals who, let's say, projected an enrollment of 1,000 students but only had 950 on October 31 found they had overspent and would be subject to budget penalties the next school year. In a moderately sized school of 1,500–2,000 students, about 17 students equaled the budget equivalent of one teacher. So, if there was an over-calculation of 34 students, the principal would owe the district the monetary equivalent of two teachers the next year.

Title I federal funding was and still is an animal all its own. As of this writing, funding is dependent on obtaining a designated percentage of students qualifying for a free lunch. If this percentage is achieved (usually somewhere between 65 percent and 73 percent), the principal receives funding. In larger schools, such funding pays for up to 10 percent of the pedagogical staff. If, in any given year, a school does not reach the cut-off point, all this funding is lost. In districts with sympathetic superintendents, the superintendent can use discretionary funding to help soften the blow, but this means that schools that do meet the Title I cut-off point can expect less than their fair share of supplementary funding from the district.

In summary: In mid-spring, principals project their enrollments. The number crunchers at the district office inform them that, based on their projections, the principals' schools can expect to be funded at X percent of full funding. The number crunchers provide them with a tentative budget allocation. The principals can now estimate how many teachers they will need and declare their vacancies.

Principals of large schools know there will be more vacancies than projected because the unexpected always happens over the summer. Teachers expected to return in the fall, don't. One decides to retire on August 31 (in many districts, teachers do not have to inform principals when they are retiring and may file for retirement at any time). Another is having a baby and needs to go on maternity leave sooner than expected. A third discovers the grass is greener as a casino dealer in Las Vegas.

As these principals review resumes and interview idealistic young adults completing university programs or entering alternative certification programs, they know they will need to have some as backups for unanticipated vacancies. At the same time, they want to be fair to these people who need jobs in the fall and not to promise them positions they may not have.

Ms. Valletta, the principal of Manhattan High School, had a relatively simple method to address this paradox. She would tell a promising applicant that she was almost sure she had a position for him, but that neither she nor any other principal in the district could promise anything definite. If he found a definite job, he should take it, but before committing, call her to let her know. If, at that time, she could make a commitment, she would. This method was fair to all parties. In many subject areas there were surplus teachers, so Ms. Valletta knew not all would find jobs and that she would have someone available in September.

It's late August. School will open in a few days. Fortunate principals know who is transferring in. They know who will not be returning to their schools. They know whom they will hire and have sent these prospective teachers to the district office to be processed. They mistakenly think their staffs are set. Other schools in the district have lost enrollment; they must now excess teachers who were on staff the previous spring. A few schools see that their projections for October 31 were too high; they excess staff so that they are not exceeding their budgets. According to the union contract, the district must place teachers in excess before permitting new teacher appointments.

In addition, some principals manipulate their budgets to excess teachers they don't want but are too lazy to rate incompetent. Every principal knows an excessed math or science teacher is suspect because no sane principal would excess a competent teacher in these shortage areas. The district knows the vacancies declared by every principal. If a principal has a vacancy for which the district has an excessed teacher, the teacher now belongs to that principal. The idealistic college graduate the principal hired just got "bumped."

Under these circumstances, some principals felt they had no control over these factors and just gave up. They let the district handle their hiring and accepted as a fait accompli that they would get transfers, excesses, and staff from the district. Competent, knowledgeable principals did not accept this. They wanted control over hiring and did all they could to gain this control.

Let's look at the union transfer plan again, this time through the eyes of an urban principal, Mr. Thelen, who did not accept getting staff members from other schools sight unseen. He had several advantages over his colleagues. First, he had a school in Manhattan which had virtually no designated parking spaces. Teachers who enjoyed driving to school (common in the outer boroughs of Queens, the Bronx, Staten Island, and parts of Brooklyn) typically would not transfer to a Manhattan school, reducing the number who would even look at vacancies there.

Second, his school was an academic-vocational school. Students in the school had to meet all the academic requirements of students in a comprehensive high school as well as the requirements of an occupational concentration. This course of study was more rigorous than the course of study in a traditional academic high school. However, most academic teachers looking to transfer didn't realize this and generally ignored schools with large vocational programs as somehow being second-rate.

Third, when it came time to list half of his projected vacancies for the union transfer list, Mr. Thelen could often list vacancies in areas in which only teachers in his school had certification. The list for his school might have vacancies in "Design and Construction of Women's Garments" or "Window Display." He knew no one could apply for these positions for there simply was no one not already in his school with these esoteric certifications. As a result, he had few union transfers.

Every school has advantages and disadvantages. Principals operating under systems with seniority transfer plans need to look at the unique aspects of their schools to determine how they can be used to mitigate these plans.

Mr. Thelen's predecessor, Principal Brown, had other creative ways of dealing with transfers. When a transfer teacher reported to his office, he would, literally, throw a tantrum. He'd yell and scream. He'd pick up the phone and call the district office and explain, in colorful language, how he had no such vacancy and could not use the so-and-so now in his office. The transfer teacher, sitting in his anteroom, could hear this harangue.

If there was no immediate reprieve, Principal Brown would have the transfer teacher sit outside his office for a few days—or even two weeks—with no assignment. If the teacher persevered, he gave him the worst program that could be constructed in terms of class preps and room assignments. Of course, the tantrum and phone call was all an act and the program a ploy. It was the rare teacher who actually stayed, as none wanted to work for such a seemingly insane and belligerent principal. Unfortunately, those few who persevered began with a negative image of the principal and school, one that tainted future professional relationships.

Mr. Thelen used a gentle variation on his predecessor's method of dealing with the few transfers he received for he wanted to build a positive relationship with his teachers, even those sent to him sight unseen. If a transfer reported to him, he would welcome her and engage her in a conversation about her previous position and experience. Sometimes, a transfer could be an excellent addition to the staff. Mr. Thelen found that roughly half of such transfers were fine professionals who sought a way out of a bad situation. He also found that some who had poor credentials had never been trained in their previous schools. He treated them as new teachers and gave them the training to become competent teachers.

Mr. Thelen did use one negative stratagem. After all, he wanted as much control over hiring as possible. After a genial welcome, a chitchat, a little history of his school, Mr. Thelen explained that in an academic-vocational school, everyone had to be flexible and sometimes teach a class out of certification. For example, the current program he had for this transferred English teacher included a class in marketing. Not to worry: The assistant principal of the marketing program would work closely with her, meet with her daily, provide materials, and observe and assist her frequently.

Sometimes, the transfer decided that an academic-vocational school might not be the best of venues and she returned to her old position. If the transfer decided to stay, however, Mr. Thelen usually managed to provide her with a revised program minus the out-of-certification class.

It pays to have a good relationship with the district's personnel officer when there are excessed teachers waiting to be placed. This was not difficult for Mr. Chen in his Brooklyn school, as both of the personnel officers he worked with were caring people who wanted the best for the schools in their district. A district and its superintendent are judged by the statistics of the schools they supervise. It is in the interest of all district personnel to help their schools succeed. Mr. Chen started off at an advantage. He had a good school whose statistics were an asset to the district. The personnel officer did not want to do anything to interfere with success. Schools at the other end of the spectrum did not get this kind of consideration.

Mr. Chen also actively assisted his district personnel officers. Part of these officers' responsibility was to organize job fairs for prospective teachers and invite schools in the district to send representatives. Mr. Chen always made sure that he attended these events. First, it was an opportunity to find teachers he might need. Second, it helped the personnel officers look good. Less than one-third of the district's schools were represented at a typical job fair, but the personnel officers always remembered who was there and who supported them. This memory came into play when it came time to place excessed teachers.

Mr. Chen also helped the borough personnel officers by finding his own teachers in hard-to-staff areas and not nagging them to find a biology or mathematics teacher. He did this by treating all applicants for a job in his school professionally. Beginning in April, Mr. Chen began receiving scores of resumes from students soon to graduate from traditional education programs. He had his secretary respond to every resume, using a simple form letter:

> Thank you for your interest in teaching at my school. At the present time, I do not anticipate any vacancies in your area. However, I will keep your resume on file for one year and contact you for an interview should such a vacancy materialize.

His secretary would skim all resumes. She would tag any that had spelling or grammatical errors; likewise, she would positively tag any that were in pristine condition. Mr. Chen then reviewed the resumes and sent any that looked promising to the appropriate assistant principal, with a note that he or she might want to contact the applicant for an interview, even if there was no projected position at the present time.

If the assistant principal conducted an interview and found the applicant to be very promising, he or she was brought to Mr. Chen's office for a follow-up interview. His canny secretary would appraise any applicant brought to the office to determine if he or she were professionally attired and "worthy" of an interview with the principal. The old adage is usually true: You can judge a book by its cover.

Mr. Chen assisted applicants who came for interviews without the promise of a position. If there was, indeed, a probable position and his budget could pay for it, he would send the candidate to the district for processing and assignment to his school. If there was no probable position, he would thank the candidate for her time, let her know that he would keep a record of the interview on file in case a position opened up, and, finally, give her a candid critique of her interview responses so she could give better interviews in the future.

Mr. Chen also worked with a group of colleagues who formed a mutual assistance society. If any of them interviewed someone they felt would be a good teacher but for whom they had no position, they would call the others to see if they had any needs.

By using this professional method for screening applicants, Mr. Chen took some control over staffing. He was able to staff his own school and save the district personnel officers the trouble of finding teachers. This was appreciated. The personnel officers knew that other principals did not devote time to finding their own teachers, so they would be the first to benefit from excessed staff.

To avoid getting excessed teachers, Mr. Chen engaged in other machinations. When Mr. Chen found a good candidate to fill a position, he called the personnel officers and asked if there were any teachers in excess in the certification area. If they said no, he sent the candidate for processing and assignment. If they said yes, he closed the prospective vacancy and inquired how many excessed teachers were waiting for assignment. Mr. Chen then arranged for the applicant to serve as a day-to-day sub in his school covering the classes of the closed vacancy until such time as all excessed teachers in the certification area had been placed. Then he reviewed his budget capability and determined that he did need another teacher. He opened the vacancy and sent his candidate to be processed and assigned. This was not as underhanded as it sounds. The district personnel officers knew what he and other savvy principals were doing. In most cases, they just ignored it.

On rare occasions, the personnel officer called Mr. Chen and said that he had to assign an excessed teacher to his school. He had no choice. Mr. Chen just accepted it and said, "Okay, but you owe me one." Good principals know when to be a team player.

Let's now look at the hiring process under a new set of circumstances in today's world of principal accountability. A district cannot hold principals accountable if it places procedural and contractual restrictions on their right to hire their own staff. In many school districts, principals got what they wanted: the end of the transfer plan as it existed, the end of being compelled to take excessed staff, and nearly total control over hiring. With new responsibilities come new challenges.

Several years ago the New York City school district gave principals more authority over hiring. They were required to create a Human Resources Committee that included teachers and administrators. This committee would decide which applicants to interview and make hiring recommendations to the principal. However, the principal made the final decision.

The requirement for a committee is the district's nod to collaboration and shared decision making within the school, although it is clear the principal makes the final decision. The use of such a committee is becoming standard in school districts around the country. On the surface this seems to be a good deal of extra work, but principals should realize that such committees help them legitimize staffing decisions, providing they establish and properly train the members of the Human Resources Committee.

The committee established by the principal should be fairly large and should represent all subject areas or grade levels in the school. Not all members will be involved in all interviews; for example, if the school is looking for a third grade teacher, the principal might involve current second, third, and fourth grade teachers, the supervisor of the third grade, and the union representative. In this way, those most affected by the hiring decision will have a voice in who is hired. This approach also means that not all members of the committee will need to be available for every interview.

Once principals have established their committees and determined their membership, it is their responsibility to train committee members so all are committed to hiring the very best applicants. An asset hired reflects positively on the school and the entire staff. A problem hired is a problem for all. In general, principals should help all committee members to agree that they must seek to hire applicants who will

- Improve student achievement and improve the school's statistics. These two items are not the same. In today's world of accountability, if teachers improve student achievement without obtaining good student statistics, they are not doing their jobs. If they obtain good test statistics but are not really educating students (because they are teaching to the test), they are not fulfilling their responsibilities. The committee must seek professionals who do not see these two ends as mutually exclusive. Teachers who truly educate students will also improve their performance on standardized tests.
- Work well with the staff of the school—colleagues, supervisors, secretaries, paraprofessionals, aides, school security agents, etc. Every school has its own unique culture, and part of the committee's job is to determine if applicants fit into the existing culture and will enhance this culture. They need to realize that they may interview very good teachers who just may

not do well in their school, although they may do very well in another school with a different culture.
- Not cause "union" issues. This is a difficult qualification to convey, particularly when a union representative will be on the committee. When a school works as a symbiotic whole, the details of the union contract are secondary to the professional responsibility to educate children. As long as the administration is concerned about the welfare and morale of staff and observes the spirit of the contract, such details usually do not cause problems.

Some applicants, depending on their prior experience, might present themselves as legal experts on the contract who will raise issues with every administrative decision. Such an applicant will be a thorn in the side of the principal and the union representative (who will have to devote substantial time to grievance hearings) and will be a negative force in the school.

(A note on contract details: No principal should ignore a contract. It is the principal's responsibility to uphold the bargaining agreement. Many current contracts are often of book length because in the past some principals were incompetent and forced the union to include protections against such incompetence. But slavish adherence to a contract hurts everyone.)

Middle school principal Ms. Hildebrand once had a teacher who, after a divorce, was having child care issues. Teachers in the school were on an early (period 1 to 8) or late (period 2 to 9) schedule. This teacher could not get to the school in time for period 2, so Principal Hildebrand made arrangements for her to work periods 3 to "10." All her classes would be held between periods 3 and 9. She would then stay in the school one period beyond the end of the late session schedule to rate papers, call parents, and tutor students.

The by-the-book union representative brought a grievance because the principal had established a new school time schedule without submitting it to the faculty for a vote. Ms. Hildebrand tried to explain that she did this to help a union member without making her personal affairs public, but being a stickler for the details of the contract, the union representative didn't care. The teacher involved was incensed at her own union representative and made sure the entire staff knew what was happening. Public opinion won the day and the representative did not pursue this.
- Work well with students and parents. The committee must try to determine if the applicant is a dedicated and caring professional whose first priority is the welfare and instruction of students and who sees parents as partners in the education of their children.

- Grow professionally and be an asset to the school. This is difficult to determine, but the committee needs to probe to find out how applicants are continuing their own educations; how their avocations may inform and enhance their teaching; and how the applicants will benefit the students and school beyond their work in the classroom.

These are the generic givens for any applicant seeking to be a teacher in the school. In addition, appropriate members of the committee, working with additional teachers and supervisors, need to establish particular criteria for specific positions. What specific criteria are being looked for in a fourth grade teacher or in a high school mathematics teacher? For each particular position, the committee needs to determine additional criteria depending upon the needs of the school at any given moment.

For example, the school may have generic and specific criteria for an art teacher. The school may also need a teacher who can organize and supervise an annual art exhibition or student variety show or multicultural day event. This will be added as a position-specific criterion for the position.

All these criteria could be applied to the resume review to determine who among the applicants will actually be called for an interview. As committee members will be giving their time, they might want to provide the principal with these criteria and allow the principal to review the resumes and make recommendations as to who should be interviewed.

Before the applicants arrive, the committee should develop a set of questions to determine how well the applicants meet the criteria that have been determined. These questions should be job specific and should relate to the uniqueness of the school. The committee should assume that anyone interested in working at the school will, at the very least, be familiar with the school's mission, student population, and statistics. This information is available online in most school districts.

The committee might also want to go beyond the traditional interview and include an on-demand writing sample on an educational issue, rated by members of the committee for literacy and content. They might want the applicants to teach a lesson to be evaluated by a subcommittee. During the summer, when students are not in attendance, applicants could be required to teach a mock mini-lesson for members of the committee. The committee might also want to see some documentation, as recommendations from colleagues and university professors and, for teachers with prior experience, copies of observation reports or letters of commendation.

Finally, the committee needs to develop a rubric to rate the applicants interviewed. Perhaps each member could use a scale from 1 to 10 to rate how well the applicant meets all the criteria for the position. Whatever criteria the committee decides upon, all applicants called for an interview should be subjected to the same evaluative process. If there is to be a mock lesson, all applicants should teach the same lesson to a similar audience. If a series of questions is generated by the committee, all applicants should be asked the same questions in the same order.

The committee members will be doing a great deal of work, especially in the initial stages; however, as part of the training process, principals must make it clear that the final hiring decision rests with the principal because the principal is ultimately accountable for the success of the school. Principals who train their committees well should find that they are almost always on the same wavelength. Perhaps a good procedure would be for the committee to recommend at least two candidates for an interview with the principal, indicating which one they felt was the more qualified, but always understanding that the principal makes the final decision.

In the real world, all this might be a moot point. With the current shortage of teachers, particularly for middle school positions and in the subject areas of special education and science, there may be few candidates to interview. The committee and the principal might have to consider not who is best for a position, but rather, whether they can live with an applicant rather than have no one.

Another issue is one of timing. Committee members may be available in April, May, and June, but not in July or August when more accurate information on enrollment and retirements becomes available. If it is mid-August and a principal cannot find a sufficient number of committee members to come in to the school on short notice, she may have to just interview applicants herself. It is more important to fill vacancies and have teachers for the children than to wait for committee members to be available and thereby lose good applicants to other schools. The principal should have the total trust of the committee that she will do what is best for the school.

The final phase for applicants is an interview with the principal. In many schools, this is the only phase, as there would be no Human Resources Committee. If this is the case, the principal should follow the same guidelines in setting generic, grade- and subject-specific, and position-specific criteria. Even if no formal committee is required by the district, the principal should involve appropriate staff in the development of these criteria and may even have some join in the interview.

As both assistant principal and principal, Ms. Niles-Perry found the following questions useful in determining if she wanted an applicant as a teacher in her school:

1. What was the best lesson you taught?
2. Why do you think this lesson worked so well?
3. What was the worst lesson you taught?
4. What went wrong with this lesson?
5. What did you do during your unassigned time at the school?
6. How would you motivate a lesson on _____?
7. What was the best suggestion made by your mentor teacher?
8. What was the worst suggestion made by your mentor teacher?
9. What do you see yourself doing five years from now?
10. If you were given a class of _____ in your program, how would you respond?
11. Why do you want to teach in this school?
12. What questions would you like to ask me about this school?
13. Why should I hire you instead of the other 10 people I am interviewing?
14. What was the last book you read for your own pleasure?
15. What magazines or journals do you read regularly? Tell me about an article you read that you think you could use in your teaching.
16. If I were to look at your Facebook page, what would I find?
17. Tell me about the (elementary, middle, or high) school you went to.
18. Which of your teachers most inspired you to go into teaching?
19. Describe any experiences you have had with inclusion classes.
20. What is your weakness as a teacher?
21. What is one trait every teacher should have?

She was trying to judge if the applicant was a reflective practitioner, could take criticism and could be flexible. Questions relating to the specific subject or grade level criteria would supplement these.

Principals should be proactive in increasing the pool of potential applicants so that they and/or a committee can make a choice and not have to settle on a less than appropriate applicant just to fill a position. Here are some strategies:

- Market the School. As previously mentioned, Principal Chen was honest about the possibilities of a position with all candidates interviewed.

He provided candidates with a critique of the interviews they gave. If he determined that the applicant would make a good addition to his staff, he began to sell his school and stress that at his school, he would provide all the support a new teacher needs. In general, there are more positions available than first-rate candidates to fill them. Principals need to market themselves and their schools.

- Maintain a Good Website. In today's technological world, more and more candidates are shopping for positions by reviewing information available on district and school websites. The better the impression these websites make on applicants, the more applicants a principal will have. Principals need to make sure their school website highlights special aspects of their programs and the achievements of their students. They need to devote staff time to updating the website often. The website is a marketing tool.
- Network with Colleagues. At workshops and retreats, principals have lunch or dinner together. They exchange information and share successes and failures. They also share information on prospective teachers. If, due to budget issues, principals must excess good teachers, they can try to place them with other members of this informal network. If someone has interviewed a good prospect but has no position, this principal will ask if anyone else could use the teacher. This informal group will expand to e-mails and telephone calls during the hiring season.
- Network with the District Personnel Officer. It is likely that every school district, large or small, has someone in the district office who serves as a contact person for applicants for positions within the district. In larger districts, the personnel officer might organize "hiring halls." As previously described, a principal needs to work professionally with the district personnel officer. When such a principal calls him in need of a teacher, the personnel officer will try to send someone who fits the culture of the school. At the end of the school year, the savvy principal will send a commendatory letter to the personnel officer with a copy to the school board or superintendent.
- Accept Student Teachers. Principals should allow local colleges to place student teachers in their schools. They should provide their best staff members as mentor teachers. Today's student teachers could become tomorrow's staff members. One caution! Principals need to be wary of schools of education that teach candidates one method to the exclusion of all others. Graduates of such programs often think they know it all. Principals want to hire teachers who are open minded. They want to train them in the culture and procedures of their own schools.

Whether the hiring of new staff is a purely administrative responsibility or one shared by a personnel committee, the above strategies will increase the number of applicants applying for positions at a school, providing that school with a real choice of applicants.

This new world of principals having control over hiring is not without issues. Those that exist in the NYC school district are representative.

A union transfer list still exists, but those on it have no right to a particular position in a particular school. They must go through the same interview process as other applicants. Excessed teachers are still awaiting assignments, but the schools they are referred to do not have to hire them or even interview them. It sounds like nirvana, but changes always create new issues. Now, a teacher hired is a teacher in the school until retirement.

The district concession to the union for the elimination of the old seniority transfer provision was a hefty pay increase and what amounts to a no-layoff clause. Teachers hired are guaranteed positions as long as they provide satisfactory service. The district had a plan to assign teachers who were laid off by schools with reduced budgets. They reported to the district office. There, a personnel officer would send them to schools with declared vacancies for interviews. If no job offers were forthcoming, they would be assigned to a school as a permanent substitute teacher. At first, the district, not the school, paid the cost of this teacher.

In the past, excessing a staff member was a way to remove a less than satisfactory teacher without going through the rigmarole of an Unsatisfactory rating. As schools with vacancies had to accept teachers in excess, these teachers found positions. Principals who didn't hire them in the first place now had to go through the Unsatisfactory rating process or figure out a way to excess them the next semester. (Of course, not all excessed teachers were unsatisfactory.)

With the new system of empowerment for principals, it becomes ethically inappropriate to excess poor teachers. The onus for additional training and, if that fails, the Unsatisfactory rating process, falls on the shoulders of the principals who hired the teacher. If this does not happen, the system will find itself with more and more excessed teachers that no one wants to hire. This then becomes a budgetary albatross that will come back to haunt the budgets of all schools. This is exactly what happened in NYC and serves as a reminder to all school districts that they must insure that principals discontinue and not excess the unsatisfactory teachers they hire. Eventually, districts will also resort to a process whereby the salary of an excessed teacher will be paid by the school until the teacher finds a placement.

A consequence of this responsibility to rate and discontinue incompetent teachers is that principals who do not understand that their job is to train teachers expect new hires to enter their schools as master teachers. If they see poor instruction, instead of training the staff, they rate them unsatisfactory and discontinue them. In the NYC school district at least, this unprofessional attitude is supported by the district which looks askance at principals who rate too few teachers as unsatisfactory. In another bureaucratic contradiction, principals who eschew their professional responsibilities for training staff are praised for "U" rating them.

If the strategies in this chapter have helped you, you will have the staff you want when your school opens in September. Finding staff is only a first step. Now you need to make sure you retain the new teachers you devoted so much time to finding.

Chapter Five

Training and Retaining New Teachers: The Critical First Week

Once principals hire the right staff, they need to train and retain them. These two—training and retaining—are intimately connected. It has been well documented that a large percentage of teachers leave the profession within five years. Some of this has to do with matters beyond the control of school leaders, such as relocation due to a spouse's job. However, many leave because school leaders do not fulfill their critical responsibility to train them to succeed. There are principals and assistant principals who see their jobs mainly as firing whomever they consider incompetent, failing to realize that this incompetence results from their own dilatory attitudes.

In today's world, many teachers come out of alternative certification programs lacking any student teaching experience. Much of their summer "indoctrination" course work is theoretical, leaving them with little practical knowledge on how to approach their first year as teachers. The training and support provided by school leaders during this first year is crucial to the success and retention of these and all newly assigned teachers.

Unfortunately, with the multitude of tasks required of school leaders, many lose sight of this primary responsibility. This is especially true for new school leaders who themselves often lack training on how to prioritize the demands they face. In some school systems, new school leaders have little teaching experience themselves and are far from the master teachers they should be. In this and the next two chapters, we will look at the experiences of Ms. Valletta, principal of Manhattan High School in Chelsea. Over time, she developed a training program for new teachers which may provide strategies and ideas to other school leaders seeking to create a professional development program for new teachers.

When Ms. Valletta first became an assistant principal in an urban school, she was lax regarding the training of her new teachers. She did the usual orientation and assigned veteran staff members as "buddies" to her new teachers. She made the observation process a meaningful staff development experience. After her first few years on the job, she could refer teachers to a departmental file which would help them with lesson planning and testing materials. She thought this was enough. Perhaps it would have been under different circumstances; however, in many schools, the staff development provided by assistant principals is really the only help given new teachers. The required district-wide workshops were neither school specific nor reality based.

Shortly before Ms. Valetta became a principal, one of Ms. Valletta's sounding-board teachers described how she had felt lost during her first year as a teacher, despite the strategies described above. Ms. Valletta thought back to her own first year as a teacher in New York City in the early 1970's. The district then required that new teachers complete a series of workshops to help them in their first year. At her school, this was organized by the assistant principal/administration to insure new teachers understood their responsibilities and were aware of the roles of key personnel in the school, many of whom came to different sessions as guest presenters.

As principal of Manhattan High School, Ms. Valletta began developing new teacher workshops loosely based on what she remembered from her own first year as a teacher and her prior experience as an assistant principal. She arranged for her workshops to earn most of the professional development hours required of new teachers. However, unlike the generic sessions periodically offered by the district, hers were designed specifically for her school and students. Over the years, she revised and expanded their content to better respond to the needs of new teachers and changes in curriculum, testing, and procedures. These workshops went beyond addressing the immediate pedagogical needs of newly assigned staff to include topics that would encourage teachers to stay with the school and see education as their life-long profession.

These staff development workshops are a primer designed to help new teachers succeed. Specific details on selected pedagogical methods are included to review some of the basics for those readers who may have fallen into the trap of forgetting what it was like to be a teacher or who may have achieved leadership positions before becoming master teachers. The topics have immediate relevancy to almost any middle or high school. They will have to be somewhat adapted to meet the needs of the elementary school.

This chapter will provide a comprehensive description of the first workshop, designed to prepare new staff to meet the critical challenges of the first day and first week of teaching. Chapter 6 will describe how this training continues in the fall semester. Chapter 7 will center on the spring semester training.

The first workshop took place on the first day teachers reported to school. While the subject area assistant principals worked with their experienced staff, the principal held a two-hour session with the newly assigned teachers, including those who had previous teaching experience but were new to the school. The latter had the option to attend future sessions. The new teachers met in the principal's conference room. All present were asked to tell the group about themselves and their prior teaching experiences, if any. Alternative certification is not a new concept. Before today's formal programs existed, many teachers were hired with no prior training under "preliminary" certification programs.

Ms. Valletta talked about herself and told the story of the double-period "honors" college-bound class she had during the first two periods of the day during her first year as a teacher. She took the class designation at face value. Her discipline was lax from day one and the students ran all over her for the entire school year. Fortunately, she was never observed in this problem class because her department supervisor taught during these same two periods.

She explained that she made two serious mistakes with this class: She tried to be a friend rather than a teacher; and when things started to go wrong, she did not immediately seek help. As a result, she had a year of misery during her first two periods. This first session of Ms. Valletta's workshop was designed to help her new teachers avoid this situation.

The first half of the workshop was devoted to planning for the first day and first week of classes, a crucial time when the tone for the entire year is determined. Ms. Valletta gave her new teachers the following guidelines:

- Teach a great lesson on the first day. Most teachers spend Day 1 on "administrivia": signing in, information card completion, seat assignments, etc., boring students to death. She told these new teachers to forget the administrivia. Quickly take attendance using the class list; then, teach a well-planned, motivating lesson that would serve as an introduction to the first unit of instruction.

The principal facilitated a discussion on how this could be done, eliciting ideas on possible topics in different subject areas and grade levels. As the new teachers would be meeting with their subject area supervisors later in the day, she advised them to discuss their first day plans with him or her. This first lesson would begin with a short assignment on the board (the "do-now") so students would begin working as soon as they entered the class. It would end with a homework assignment, clearly written on the board for students to copy.

The advice to teach a great lesson on the first day proved so successful with these new teachers that the following September Ms. Valletta made it a part of her opening remarks at the staff development faculty conference. She received more positive feedback from her staff for this one simple idea than for any other piece of advice dispensed at a general conference.

- To teach a good lesson, you need a good motivation. The principal and her new teachers briefly discussed how to motivate instruction. This is more fully discussed in the spring workshop described in chapter 7.
- Do not tell the students about yourself. This is the "I am your friend" trap that new teachers fall into. One of the great advantages teachers have is the mystery that surrounds them. All students, middle and high school students especially, have an innate curiosity about their teachers (some believe teachers are born fully formed and have no lives outside the school). This aura of mystery carries with it a mantle of authority that teachers should exploit. Yes, some facts about teachers will be revealed as they teach, but this will be piecemeal and only add to the questions students have about their teachers.
- Do not give students the "class rules." Simply enforce them as the need arises. Ms. Valletta elaborated:

On Day 1, have a late sheet by the door. If students enter after the late bell, have them sign the late sheet. At the end of the class, remind students that you expect them to be on time every day. You will be flexible today, as they are dealing with new programs and class changes. However, tomorrow, you will be calling the parents of late students. Follow up on this and all promises.

When entering students start to congregate around your desk for a variety of reasons—not sure if they are in the right class, they have health problems you need to know about, they need a pass—tell them to sit down and begin working on the assignment written on the board. Then, circulate as they are working and handle these issues.

If a student requests a bathroom pass at the beginning of the lesson, simply say, "There are no passes the first 10 minutes of this class." Once an interesting lesson begins, most students forget they need to use the bathroom. After 10 minutes when a persistent student asks for the bathroom pass, provide him with the heavy wooden block for your room (one of Ms. Valletta's teachers was married to a carpenter who graciously provided these) and then have him sign the pass book, recording the time leaving and, when he comes back, the time of return. Inform students no one else may leave until he returns with the class pass.

If a student calls out an answer during the lesson, simply say, "We do not call out answers in this class; please raise your hand—and, for the next few days, tell me your name before you respond so I can quickly learn who you are."

All of these procedures are designed to deal with the Day 1 testing of the teacher by the students. They let students know that the usual games will not work in this class.

- Be organized. Organization equals improved management. The board organization of the first day will be the organization for the semester: Do-now to the right, homework to the left, and the middle left open for an organized summary of the major topics of the lesson.

Your desk will be neat and not piled with papers just waiting to waft to the floor. On the first day, you will have paper for students who do not bring any. You will have a supply of large pens (the bigger the better) for students who need them. The difference between a new and an experienced teacher is that the new teacher is constantly buying more pens as his pens loaned to students are not returned; the experienced teacher ends the semester with more pens than when she began.

As students enter, tell them they are not to sit in the first row or the row nearest the door. Only fill these seats if necessary. During the next few days, new students arriving late from their summer vacations will report. You can seat these in the row by the door and sign them in as the rest of the class works on the opening assignment. At the end of the week, you can ask if any students have difficulty seeing the board or hearing your comments. You can then move these to the first row without displacing other students. You can also use first row desks for students you think may be troublesome.

Another aspect of organization is having a folder for each class where you can put collected homework, quizzes, and tests. In this way, you will not misplace materials or confuse materials from different classes. Of course, all papers are rated and returned the next day.

Have an Absent/Late folder for each class near the late-sign-in sheet by the door. Students who enter late (after you have returned papers) should know to check this folder for their work. Students absent the previous day will know their work is in the folder so there will be no need to go your desk to ask for returned assignments.

- Dress as the role model of a professional. There has been a deterioration of professional dress in this country. This is disturbing. For a serious business, serious dress should be required. Education is serious business, and one way a school and its teachers project this is by dressing professionally.

Teachers are role models for how adults dress in the real world and may be the only such role models in their students' lives. New high school teachers may not be much older than the students they are teaching. Professional dress and hair styling separate them from their students. No matter how helpful or friendly you may be, you must maintain this separation.

All teachers must remember which side of the desk they are on. Because dress is a civil liberty, a principal may not be proscriptive with new teachers or any teachers in the school. However, Ms. Valletta would comment on the professional demeanor and persona of teachers in observation reports. Professional, adult dress equals an aura of authority and provides a better ambience for a well-managed classroom.

- During the first week, give homework every night, collect it every day, and return it with comments the next day. The principal advised these new teachers to warn their significant others that they would have little free time during their first year of teaching and probably would collapse on the sofa with physical and mental fatigue when they got home. She assured them it got easier every year. The principal gave each workshop participant a homework log sheet (one created by a teacher in the school) and explained its use (see figure 5.1).

This log made students responsible for keeping homework records. Each day, the teacher would update the log posted on the class bulletin board. Any absent student who missed a homework assignment could check the log and know what he or she had to do. In more recent versions of this workshop, Ms. Valletta advised teachers to post this log online. Absent students would be expected to check this and have all their assignments when they returned to class.

HOMEWORK LOG   CLASS: TEACHER:

DATE GIVEN	DATE DUE	DESCRIPTION OF ASSIGNMENT	DATE RETURNED	SCORE
		(This was a full page with about 20 spaces)		

Figure 5.1. Homework Log Sheet.

- Call parents every evening. During the first week, make it a point to call the parents of several students in each class—students who were late, did not turn in assignments, or were unruly. Soon, every student in the class will know you call parents. After the first week, you can relax this a bit, but always try to call at least one parent each night. The call could be a positive one, such as to say Maria had a 95 on the test you gave this week.
- If you have a problem, seek help immediately. Small issues not addressed the first week become major issues as the school year progresses.

There are things you can do in the classroom to defuse issues. Always be an adult role model and never lower yourself to the level of an angry or disturbed child. Stay calm. Never raise your voice. Never challenge a child before his or her peers; talk to the child privately during or after class. Never take spiteful remarks or foul language personally.

Ms. Valletta gave a thumbnail summary of Adolescent Psychology I. These are adolescents going through the most difficult time of their lives, facing pressures for peer acceptance, for sex, for drugs, for gangs. They can be explosive as the pressures on them build. Teachers must understand this and if such explosions happen, stay calm and defuse. This rarely happens early in the semester when most students are on their best behavior during the test-the-teacher period. The students are trying to figure you out and see what they can get away with in your class.

During the first weeks, if you are organized and firm and if you follow the previous advice, there should be few, if any, problems. If an issue does arise, see your subject area supervisor immediately for advice and help. He or she will know exactly how to handle any problem. If you find this is not the case, see the principal.

The second half of this first session was less intense. Principal Valletta began with some advice on interpersonal relations. She told her new teachers that schools are hierarchal institutions. Within the teaching staffs of school departments, seniority is the main factor in determining who is at the top. In the past, some new teachers, fresh from the university, felt they knew more about teaching than the veterans. Some, having been in managerial or even executive positions prior to entering alternative certification programs, felt they could run a school better than the principal. Such attitudes are guaranteed to alienate the experienced members of the staff. She warned her new teachers that until they prove themselves as pedagogues, they are at the bottom of the hierarchy and should keep such opinions to themselves.

She also told them that school leaders and master teachers often judge newcomers by the company they keep. She advised them to seek out the most respected members of their departments. Ask their advice. Have lunch with them. Learn from them. These master teachers, whether formally assigned as mentors or buddies or not, will be willing to help them. On the other hand, every school has its malcontents. They congregate together, criticize the school leaders and complain about their colleagues and students. Avoid this group. If you are unsure which staff members fall into each category, ask your department supervisor or principal.

Principal Valletta then distributed the *Teacher Handbook* and briefly commented on several items included in it. She advised her teachers to read it from cover to cover during the first week. She stressed the section on legal matters, noting that violating any of the district regulations could lead to dismissal. Ms. Valletta explained her observation policy and informed these new teachers that she would visit one of their classes the next day. She provided them with their professional period assignments, to assist their assistant principals in the management of their offices. She wanted to give each a daily opportunity to talk with their immediate supervisors.

Ms. Valletta described the school ambience that she, as principal, tried to promote. She stressed that she wanted to make this school a safe and structured place where every student knew what was expected. She added that all staff members were expected to respect students, parents, and colleagues even if, sometimes, the respect was not returned. Most major problems and issues are avoided when staff members show respect and care. Anger and angst result when this is lacking.

She provided teachers with the dates of the fall workshops, scheduled around the times when she knew she would be out of the building for various conferences. The principal stressed that all dates were tentative, as emergencies sometimes happened.

She gave participants a copy of the *Student Handbook* so they would be aware of the information being given to students and their parents. They were asked to become familiar with this information, especially if they were scheduled to teach any freshman classes as their students would ask them questions and expect them to have the answers. She directed them to the diagram of the school in the handbook and advised them to take a walk around the school before they left that day to locate the main offices and locales: the auditorium, lunchroom, library, gym, student bathrooms, etc. She gave them classroom and bathroom keys.

Finally, Ms. Valletta noted that it was district and school policy that teachers provide students with a course outline during the first few weeks of the semester. For this first semester, she advised the teachers to be less than precise since, as new teachers, most would be planning day to day and then week to week. Each department had a standard form to use, so she suggested they obtain one from their department chairs. This outline had to indicate the teacher's grading method. The principal suggested that they indicate that all work done—homework, quizzes, tests and major assignments, and participation—would be incorporated into the grade. They could follow up with a more precise explanation after the fourth workshop (described in the next chapter).

All school leaders know that the first day of classes is critical to the success of new teachers. It is vital that school leaders provide new staff with the practical knowledge they need to do well on this first day of their careers. Then, as explained in the following two chapters, they need to continue to provide instruction in the practice of pedagogy for the entire school year.

Before concluding this chapter, it is appropriate to look at thoughts in the back of Ms. Valletta's mind as she planned and conducted her new teacher workshop sessions:

- This principal was trying to provide her new teachers with very practical ideas and advice. She was trying to help them become organized teachers. When she observed teachers, old and new, she saw that many worked too hard. Teaching is a difficult profession, but teachers who lack organizational skills work harder than necessary. They lose track of papers. They do not save and reuse good materials such as lesson plans, handouts, and test questions. They allow opening activities such as quizzes or do-nows to take up half the period instead of crisply completing them in a few minutes.

    Students know they cannot play games with organized teachers who establish clear classroom routines. Students like the comfort of such routines, especially if the teacher can infuse them with humor.
- Many of the items discussed during these workshops were helpful to other teachers on the staff. Where appropriate, the principal incorporated them into post-observation conferences with experienced teachers. Sometimes, a topic found its way into a general conference.

    While the training of new staff is paramount, one must also help improve the instruction provided by existing staff; however, Ms. Valletta

remembered that new teachers are still moldable while some veteran staff is moldy. It is hard to change the practices of someone who has been teaching over five years.
- New guidance counselors attended. The principal wanted them to understand what new teachers faced as the counselors fulfilled their function as child advocates. The principal also could draw upon the counselors' expertise during many of the discussions concerning discipline and dealing with difficult students. New teachers learned the role of the counselors.
- Ms. Valletta tried to provide refreshments. If there was any special event in her office, she saved the leftovers, such as cookies and coffee, for the workshop participants. On some occasions, she baked cookies. Establishing a good comfort level is important.
- An unanticipated positive resulted from the new teacher workshops. Many of the participants developed their own support group. After each session, they went to a local watering hole to relax, unwind, and continue to share their experiences. Through the session they learned they were not alone, that all new teachers, whatever level or subject, face similar problems. By discussing these problems with the principal, assistant principal, experienced teachers, and each other, they could develop a repertoire of strategies to handle almost every situation.

Chapter Six

Training and Retaining New Teachers: The Fall Semester

The training for the first day and week was only the beginning of Ms. Valletta's staff development program for new teachers. A second workshop followed a week later. This and all ensuing workshops lasted about one hour and began with the sharing of experiences and asking of questions.

The principal began the second workshop by asking her new teachers to share their reactions to being informally observed by her on the first day of classes. In general, she found that this practice eased tensions and helped her new teachers to become comfortable with observers in their classes. She described the positives and negatives of what she observed without revealing names. The opening discussion then turned to classroom management issues, as it did almost every week. After the sharing of experiences and strategies, the principal turned to the main topic of this session, handling paperwork.

Much teacher paperwork is generated by others: the school system, the immediate supervisor, the principal. Ms. Valletta told her neophytes to complete any paperwork given them quickly and correctly. Putting it aside would only force their overworked administrators to send reminders. Doing it incorrectly meant they doubled their work when they had to redo it.

Ms. Valletta recounted an anecdote from her own first day of teaching. In those days of yore, each grade advisor worked with the teachers of the homeroom classes he or she advised. This was before computers, so teachers, under the supervision of the grade advisor, handled program changes, report card books, and, at the end of the semester, the programming of students for the next semester. The paperwork associated with the homeroom class was immense. Her grade advisor was a veteran teacher, Mr. Willard. When they met to review the programs of the students in her homeroom, he told her the key to keeping her job: "Maria, no one cares if you can teach. All they care about is that your paperwork is done right and on time."

Ms. Valletta doubted the former, but she was sure he was right about the latter. In any organization, poor paperwork is a mark of incompetence. Ms. Valletta told her new teachers she had known very few master teachers who were administratively challenged; however, the poor teachers she knew invariably were incompetent with paperwork. She explained that principals and assistant principals will usually conclude that teachers who do poor paperwork probably do poorly in the classroom as well.

She then told them Mr. Willard's next comment: "Maria, always remember that every class you program or change, every grade you enter or check, every piece of paper you submit in some way affects the future of a child. An error you make now could prevent a child from graduating." Over her many years in education, she realized how right Mr. Willard was. Caring professionals remember that their paperwork affects the futures of children.

The rest of the paperwork is generated by the teachers themselves: homework, quizzes, tests, reports, and papers. The principal promised her new teachers that if they took her advice, they could cut the time spent on this paperwork in half. In this session, she would deal specifically with homework. In the next session, she would address other items.

Following her advice from the first workshop, the new teachers had been giving homework every night, collecting it, rating it, and returning it the next day. She explained that they had done this to get students into the habit of doing homework and to send the message that homework completion was important and a part of the final grade.

Now, she said, it is time to reduce your paperwork. You do not have to read and rate most homework assignments. Homework has one of two purposes: to review what was taught during the day's lesson, or to prepare students for the next day's lesson. Many assignments do both. The homework submitted tells the teacher whether or not the students are learning what is being taught. There are at least five ways a teacher may deal with homework:

- The quick check. Have students put homework on their desks while they complete the do-now. Circulate around the room and simply give students credit for completing the homework if it is there. Then, review the homework at the beginning of the period.
- The combination check. Have the student complete the do-now directly on their homework paper (no homework, no do-now accepted on this day).

Collect both. Instead of two pieces of paper, the teacher now has one. This method is especially effective when the do-now is a quiz. A variation on this method could also increase student participation. Begin the class by reviewing the homework. Ask if anyone has a question or problem. Count to 10. When no one responds, say, "Flip your homework paper over and answer the following quiz questions." When rating the work, give automatic credit for the homework and rate the quiz. You can be sure that the next time you ask for questions, many will be forthcoming.

- The spot check. Instead of rating all papers collected, rate the papers of students in one row only. This will tell you if your students understood what was taught. The students not checked get credit for the work. Vary the row selected, seemingly at random, but insuring that every row is rated equally during each marking period.
- The complete check. To keep students honest, rate an entire class's work at least once a week; vary the day.
- The no check. Do not collect, do not check; just review with the class.

Be transparent and explain these different methods to the students. The method used on any day will vary according to the type of assignment given. Students can try to second-guess you and not do an assignment on a given day. If they are wrong, they get a 0 which will negatively affect their grades.

At this point, the principal gave her new teachers a simple way to incorporate homework, quizzes, and do-nows into the grades of the students. All such items should be rated out of 10. Any student who demonstrates that he at least put some effort into the work should receive a minimum grade of 6, except on quizzes, where the grade could be as low as a 0. When the teacher has a total of eleven items, he or she should add them up for a test score out of 100. By having eleven items, each student gets one freebie, whether due to an absence, a missed assignment or just a bad day. Any work just checked gets the full 10 points.

The principal noted that different departments weigh homework differently. In English/ESL, foreign language, and social studies, for instance, it is usually a major portion of the grade (about 30 percent). In math, where the ability to solve problems is paramount, exams and quizzes are more important than homework so the latter might only be 10 percent of the grade. However, students who do not do the homework usually do not do well on tests and quizzes. Each teacher was asked to speak to his or her subject area supervisor to find out their department's policy.

The workshop attendees were asked to bring any quizzes they had used or planned to use to the next week's session.

The third new teacher workshop concerned the creation of quizzes and major tests. Here the principal relied on what she had learned in an undergraduate course in tests and measurements. Few teacher preparation programs, graduate or undergraduate, traditional or alternative, include such a course today. This is ironic as test and data interpretation is becoming a major professional responsibility. Over time, the principal updated what her teachers needed to know and incorporated information related to district testing requirements. The generic parts of the workshop are described below.

Ms. Valletta first defined two key testing terms: *validity* and *reliability*. In simple terms, *validity* means that the exam actually tests for the content and skills taught. *Reliability* means that the results on the test would be duplicated on a second testing; that is, a student who earned an 80 percent on the test should earn a similar grade on a retesting.

The principal noted that few new teachers knew how to make up good classroom examinations that would be valid and reliable. She distributed samples of full-period exams she had collected over several years. All used fill-in, true/false, or matching questions—all notoriously unreliable. The placement of the answers on the question paper made grading difficult. In one case, the exam was hand-written and unprofessional looking. In general, instructions were vague and questions open to too wide an interpretation. After discussing these materials, the principal provided her new teachers with guidelines for teacher-made exams:

- All major exams should use questions that parallel the types of questions students will face on district-required standardized examinations. Following the format of the district exams, all short-answer questions should be well-devised multiple choice questions. All essays will simulate one of the essay types of questions on the exams. All math problems will parallel the district exams in style, language, and difficulty.
- Students will have only 40 minutes for the exam. Be sure students can complete the exam during this time. In general, there should be no more than 10–20 multiple choice questions and one essay type question requiring no more than a one-page response. There should be no choice of questions.

Many departments have files of questions on different units. Standardized exam review books have past test questions. More questions are available on district and state Internet sites. You can select questions relevant to the subject matter of the exam. Adjust the language of the questions to the grade level of the students in your classes.

- Always add an extra-point question (worth no more than five points) that requires a great deal of writing or solving to keep early finishers occupied.
- The first two or three multiple choice questions should be easy. Some students, even those who are well prepared, fear exams. When they see they can easily handle the first few questions, they gain confidence.
- Always have a review session one or two days before a major exam. Include a handout with samples of multiple choice essay questions. Require students to do the essay part as a homework assignment so their work can be discussed in class. When the test day comes, students will be familiar with the format of your exam and will know the content it will cover.
- Always make your exam professional looking. Neatly word process and proofread it.
- Always have separate question papers and answer sheets. This simulates standardized exam format, helps reduce paper consumption, and guards the integrity of the exam.

If you are giving the same exam in two or three different classes, collecting the question papers prevents students in an earlier class from showing them to students in a later class. Always put the essay on a separate page and use a different essay question for each class. In general, students will not remember multiple choice questions, but will remember the one essay question.

- For the first exam given, create an A and a B version of the multiple choice part—same questions, but with the correct answers jumbled for each version. Have a prominent A or B at the top of each exam. Give each version to alternate rows. Do not tell students the meaning of the A and B. After you collect papers, you can inform students that you hoped they did not have roaming eyes, for the answers of the students next to them did not match the answers on their own tests.

After doing this once, keep using the A and B, but you will not have to redo the order of the responses. Students will assume you've done this. As time goes on and you teach the same type of class over and over again, you will develop a good e-file of questions so you can make several versions of the same test for use with different classes or rows.

NAME_____CLASS_____PERIOD_____

EXAMINATION ANSWER SHEET

Make NO marks on your question paper. All answers belong on this answer sheet. Put the answers to your multiple choice questions next to the appropriate numbers in the column to the left. Write your essay on the lines provided below. If you need more space, use the back of this paper.

1___   _____

2___   _____

3___   _____

4___   _____

5___   _____

6___   _____

7___   _____

8___   _____

9___   _____

10___   _____

(Numbers continue to "20")

Figure 6.1. Standard Answer Sheet.

- Use a standard answer sheet that will put all student work on one page and make marking easier. Ms. Valletta's school has Scantron automatic test forms and machines, but these are too costly for use in regular class exams. The principal provided the participants with a standard answer sheet (see figure 6.1).
- Rate and return the exam as quickly as possible. Review it, but not question by question. Provide students with an exemplary response to the essay or solution to a mathematical problem. Have them compare it to their own returned work. Go over any multiple choice questions that the majority of students had difficulty with. Always collect and keep the answer papers so you can use the same multiple choice questions the next year.

- Actively proctor your own exams. There would be a brief discussion of this. The proctoring of standardized examinations would be discussed in detail before the fall testing period.
- Look at the test results to determine if any questions were too difficult or too easy. Almost everyone should have gotten the first few questions correct because you designed them this way. Look for other questions on the exam that almost everyone had correct, even those who scored poorly overall. Likewise, look for questions almost everyone had incorrect, even those who scored well. Such questions poorly discriminate and need to be revised or eliminated before you use the exam again.
- While using student monitors to correct short quizzes is acceptable, the principal cautioned against this for major exams. A student's grade is private and should not be known by another student, even a trusted monitor. The marking of tests and homework is an excellent way to involve your significant other in your professional life.

Short quizzes are another matter altogether. You want to determine if students did the readings or attempted the problems assigned the previous night and/or listened in class the previous day. Their purpose is to reward effort and to have students see this as an easy way to improve their grades by simply doing the assignment. After discussing the sample quizzes participants brought to the session, the principal provided simple guidelines for quizzes:

- As your students have been trained to put their homework on the desk upon arrival, have students do quizzes right on their homework paper. Or, provide students with a half sheet of paper. Ms. Valletta used to have a stack of half sheets on her desk to signal that the day was a quiz day. As soon as the bell beginning the class rings, have the first student in each row quickly pass back the papers.

    Say, "I will ask a question; I will pause; I will repeat the question and then pause again. I will not repeat any questions at the end of the quiz." Ask the questions. After the final pause after the last question, say, "All pens down. I will count to five. Any papers not in the hands of the students in the first row by the end of the count will not be accepted." Count to five, collect the papers.

    Latecomers? They may start where they come in. As questions are not repeated at the end of the quiz, they will miss some. If they miss the entire

quiz, they receive no credit. Quizzes, for which there are no make-ups, are a good way to encourage students to arrive in class on time.
- Always stand in the back of the class looking down at the students so you can see them and they cannot see you. The principal described how she used to stand on a desk in the back of the room looking down at the class.
- In general, ask five short questions (in math, one or two problems previously written on the board). The first should be easy, such as "Who was Lady Macbeth's husband?" The next three should be slightly harder, but designed so that any student who did the reading/homework with any degree of attention should get correct answers. The last question might be more difficult and even thought provoking, such as "Why did Lady Macbeth sleepwalk?"

The goal of the quiz is to insure that the students who did the reading/homework achieve at least a 6 so that those who didn't do the work will realize they missed earning very easy credit.
- Rate each answer out of two. This allows for partial credit for a response that's close but not quite right, and avoids fractional scores or half points.
- The whole process, from paper distribution to collection, should take no more than five minutes.
- Finally, don't let students get complacent. A quiz does not have to come at the beginning of class. It could come after the homework review to see if students were paying attention and to help you determine if students had learned what was intended.

The principal advised that her new teachers use a "feedback" quiz every week or so. With about five minutes left at the end of the period, distribute paper and simply ask, "Please describe, in your own words, what you learned in class today." The student responses will help you determine the effectiveness of your lesson. This practice also makes a great "elastic ending" to lessons that run short. The students will never know you finished too early and will think the quiz was part of your plan for the day.

The workshop attendees were told to implement these guidelines for upcoming quizzes and major exams so they could report back on their experiences at future sessions.

The fourth workshop concerned how to determine student grades. This was a timely topic as first marking period grades were due in about two weeks. The principal explained that most student and parent complaints about teachers concern what they consider unfair grades. She asked if anyone had any questions about what they had read on marking and grading in the *Teacher Handbook*. She responded to these questions and then explained that there are, of course, as many methods of marking and grading as there are teachers.

Ms. Valletta wanted them to implement the suggestions in the handbook for two reasons. First, she knew they worked. She had used them during her many years in the classroom. She never had a complaint about a grade. Second, it was her responsibility to insure students were graded consistently. By training new staff in the same method, there would be greater fairness in the grades given, regardless of who taught what class.

Each semester was divided into three marking periods, each generating a report card. Each grade was cumulative. That is, the grade for the second marking period was to include all the grades for both first and second marking periods averaged together; likewise, the third and final grade, which appeared on the students' transcripts, was the cumulative average of all grades for the semester.

A teacher could manipulate grades to help students who falter early but do better as the term progresses. The first marking period usually had few grades, as there was usually only time for one major test and no reports. Most teachers had only three grades (two homework/quiz grades and one test). The second marking period would have more grades. There would be more homework and quiz scores, more tests, and, perhaps, a major assignment (such as a book report) due. These could total six or more grades. When the teacher computed a cumulative grade for the second marking period report card, the work of the second marking period would be worth double the work of the first, giving students who had started slowly a chance to do better.

The new teachers were advised to follow this logic into the third marking period. In addition to regular tests, homework and quizzes, major reports and term papers were usually due and might be given double weight because of the time and effort required to complete them. Final exams were also given. The teacher should have 10 or even 12 grades to average in from the third marking period. A student who had done poorly going into the final marking period would have the opportunity to improve and pass the class.

The principal also had a suggestion: For the final marking period, drop the two lowest grades of the semester from the average. Did a student miss an exam and not make it up? This grade (a 0) is dropped. Was a student sick for a week, missing all the quizzes and homework? This mark is dropped.

Of course, a student consistently absent or remiss in work will still have a problem. Dropping the two lowest grades will not help this student. For others, it negates the impact of an illness or short-term slump. Dropping two of over twenty grades will still lead to a fairly computed final average.

Ms. Valletta also strongly suggested that a day or two before report card distribution, each teacher give a full-period writing assignment (or the equivalent) in class to allow the teacher a chance to speak briefly with each student about his or her grade. She used to give each student a grade explanation sheet, a listing of all the grades, the average, the adjustment for participation, and the report card grade. This extra paperwork saved her the agita of grade complaints. In schools with websites accessible by students, this explanation sheet could be e-mailed and then discussed with each child individually the next day.

On report card distribution day, some teachers have major issues with class management because students are upset by "unfair" grades. If the new teachers followed her suggestion, there would be no such issue in their classes because the students would already know their grades and how they were computed.

Even with the use of well-defined rubrics, all marking of written work is, to some extent, subjective. Fortunately, students and parents usually see such marks as objective. Most often, complaints target the always subjective "participation" grade. The principal had two suggestions regarding the "participation" grade:

- First, this should never be more than plus or minus five points of the grade. Keep subjectivity to a minimum. The district's grade entry system required all grades under 90 be in multiples of five; grades over 90 would be exact. Use the participation grade to determine whether or not an in-between grade goes up or down to the nearest multiple of five. For grades over 90, keep the participation variable to an absolute minimum.
- Second, never use the participation grade to determine a failure. A student with a failing grade of 61 could earn a passing grade due to positive participation. However, a student with a passing grade of 65 should not have it reduced to a failing grade because of poor participation.

Ms. Valletta ended this session with the rule of thumb she followed throughout her teaching career: If she had any doubt as to whether a semester grade should be passing or failing, she never went wrong by erring on the side of the student. By now, several of the opening discussions had dealt with the difficult lives of students in today's world. While educators want to insure that students learn the skills and knowledge of a course's curriculum, they must remember that one semester of instruction is part of many other semesters, where spiraling instruction insures that the work of a single semester will be reviewed again.

The next workshop was added at the very end of Ms. Valletta's career. Her assistant principal/administration was now responsible for overseeing the data and all standardized test results for the school, assisted by a data/testing coordinator. These two staff members conducted the session in a computer room to make the new teachers aware of all the information now available online about their classes in general and their students in particular. The new teachers were already aware of some of this, but not all. The workshop was intended to help them maximize their understanding and use all the data at their command. For the last segment of the session, the principal led a discussion on how they could use this data to inform their instruction.

The assistant principals of the subject areas were aware of the content of their principal's workshops and supported them with their own staff development of their new teachers. For this workshop, however, the principal wanted her assistant principals to follow up with a formal session to help their new teachers learn how to use data to plan and differentiate their lessons and assessments to meet the needs of their students. While numbers do not fully describe the needs of a child, in today's world they will be used to evaluate teachers' performance and, perhaps, determine their retention and salary increases. It would be remiss of school leaders not to make sure teachers fully understand data.

Workshop number six was titled "Who Are the Most Important People in the School Building?" The principal wanted these new staff members to understand the roles of the different people in the school and appreciate their contributions to the students' success and the school's ambience. Where appropriate, she also told them the best way to approach the different staff members they might interact with.

- The usual response to "Who is the most important person in the school to you, as new teachers?" was "The principal." When Ms. Valletta disagreed, the next choice was "The custodian." Again, she disagreed to the amazement of the new teachers. She explained that to them, the most important person was her secretary.

If they had not passed her muster, they might never have gotten in to see her. Because they were hired, they can be sure that when they arrived for their interview, her secretary had given them her seal of approval: "A well-dressed and groomed intelligent-looking gentlemen (or lady) is here to see you." She rated applicants on manners, grooming, and dress. Her continued good opinion would determine if they had unlimited future access to the principal.

- The second most important person is the payroll secretary, for she makes sure teachers are paid properly, have medical coverage, and join the pension system. They had to help her by correctly filling out all the papers she gave them and returning them as soon as possible. They must keep her up-to-date on changes of status, including additional graduate credits and degrees earned. She cautioned that her school's payroll secretary would do anything she could to help a teacher who treated her courteously. But, heaven help the rare misanthrope who lacked courtesy and respect.
- Next on the list of important people is the custodial staff. Custodians tend to come and go (see chapter 11) but the staff remains the same. Most of these custodial helpers speak English poorly, but treated with respect are of great help in correcting classroom maintenance problems. Teachers needed to remember that the ability to fix a broken window or door jamb was almost as important to their classroom ambience as their ability to teach.
- For these new teachers to retain their jobs, the most important persons are their subject area assistant principals. The assistant principals will observe them often, formally and informally, and be mainly responsible for their training in their different disciplines. At the end of the year, they will recommend that the principal rate them as "Satisfactory" or "Unsatisfactory."

The task of new teachers is to listen to their supervisors' advice and implement it. The assistant principals know they are new and need to learn the art of teaching. As long as they implement suggestions and improve over the course of the year, they need not fear a negative rating. The assistant principals also serve as their advocates if some issue, such as a parent complaint, comes to the principal.

- Then, of course, there is the principal. Ms. Valletta explained that she was an unusual principal because she personally involved herself in their day-to-day training through these workshops and her own formal and informal observations of their instruction. She worked closely with their assistant principals to insure all training was consistent.

Ms. Valletta then told her new teachers what Mr. Eddy, the assistant principal who ran her own first-year training sessions, had told her: "Make yourself indispensable to the school." Even if they are good teachers, there are many variables that determine if they retain their jobs: budget restrictions, contractual transfers, teachers returning from sabbaticals. In June, even good teachers lose their jobs or are excessed to other schools.

A principal looks beyond teaching to make the difficult decisions. What else did each teacher do to help the school? Who came early and stayed late working with students? Who volunteered to help at school events? Who attended Parent Association Meetings? Who took over the supervision of a club?

The principal ended by briefly explaining the roles of other key administrators: the AP/Organization, the AP/Pupil Personnel Services, and the AP/Security. Each of these individuals would be conducting a future session to more fully describe their roles in the school.

The seventh session was not part of the original set of workshops scheduled by Ms. Valletta. She added it in her third year as principal. She titled this session "Teacher to Teacher" and invited new teachers from the previous two years to share their experiences with this year's new teachers. She specifically asked her second and third year teachers to be honest with the new group, especially as to whether or not what she was telling them in these workshops really worked. She had a great deal of confidence in herself to do this, especially since she left the room and closed the door.

She returned for the last 10 minutes for a debriefing. The one comment that almost always greeted her was how the second and third year teachers had told them how much easier these next years were. Ms. Valletta had been reminding her new teachers at almost every session that the first year was the most difficult, but it would get easier. She was not fully believed until this session when the "graduates" of her workshop program said the same thing.

The eighth session dealt with parents and upcoming parent conferences. The principal reviewed material in the *Teacher Handbook*, illustrating them with examples from her own experiences.

She explained that no amount of time would be sufficient to satisfy the eagerness of many parents for a better understanding of the progress of their children. The new teachers had to plan interview time carefully so that parents came away with the facts about their children's achievement as well as a positive feeling about the faculty, the programs, and the school. The amount of time a teacher could devote to each parent would depend on the number of parents who were waiting.

She provided the new teachers with the following suggestions:

- Have your room decorated with subject-related posters and exemplary student work.
- Be sure the standards for your subject are clearly posted.
- Establish a cooperative working relationship with parents as soon as they enter: rise to welcome them, shake hands, smile, and offer a friendly greeting. Sit facing the parent, not behind the barrier of your desk.
- Always begin with a positive comment about the child.
- Have your attendance and marking records handy. Be sure both can be easily understood. Provide clear explanations, exact dates, and assignment descriptions.
- Enlist the parents' aid in trying to find reasons for a child's deficiencies: "What can *we* do to get Jill to do her homework?" stresses the partnership of teachers and parents in helping the child. Saying "Jill never does her homework" places the parent in the position of having to defend the child.
- If you have many parents waiting in line to see you:
  - Courteously try to end the interview, noting that other parents want to learn about their children also.
  - Take the parent's phone number and call the next day to continue the interview.
  - Arrange for an additional interview with the parent during regular school hours.
  - Refer the parent to the student's guidance counselor; if a child is having trouble in one class, chances are he or she is having trouble in others as well.

The principal reminded the teachers they represent the entire staff of the school. Their dress, manner, and comments all reflect on their professionalism and the professionalism of their colleagues.

She admitted that most of the parents they would see would be the parents of students doing well. Some teachers get exasperated because they really want to see the parents of students doing poorly. Never let this happen. A main reason students succeed is the interest and involvement of their parents. Praise this parent with words such as "I'm sure you are receiving excellent reports on Mary's work. Much of her success is due to your success as a parent and your interest in her work." Such parents sacrifice their time to come to these conferences. Give them a pat on the back.

Ms. Valletta told a story from her fourth year as a teacher, when she met with the father of Josh, a high school junior. Josh was an average student, a kind and gentle boy, a bit introverted. When his father, a commercial airline pilot and obvious extrovert, came to see her, with Josh at his side, his first comment was "Well, how is my dummy doing in your class?" Ms. Valletta could see Josh cringe.

She praised her student, describing his fine manners and pleasant personality. Dad's only response was "I guess he's too stupid to go to college." She disagreed, saying he was an average student who should go to college. She advised him to speak with the College Counselor before he left for the evening. Dad was already getting up, and, as he left with Josh, he said, "Nah, I'm not going to waste my time."

The principal asked her workshop group what they would do if faced with a similar situation. All agreed that they should not confront the parent in front of the child, but that the child's guidance counselor needed to be alerted to begin an intervention. In today's world, similar comments made by a teacher would be considered verbal abuse; however, it is unlikely they fit the legal definition of "child abuse" by a parent.

She next said that on rare occasions, a parent actually slapped a child in front of her. If this were to happen, it was the teacher's responsibility to protect the child and report the parent to the child welfare agency, following the school's policy on this matter.

A few years back, in the only example of this the principal had ever known, a parent became angry at a teacher and literally climbed over the desk to try to attack her. Fortunately, Ms. Kent, an assistant principal who was walking by the room, charged in and tackled the parent before she could assault the teacher. She held the parent down until school security arrived and escorted the parent from the building. Forever after, Ms. Kent was known by the nickname, the "Manasses Mauler."

Ms. Valletta was not the principal at the time, so was not privy to all the details of this incident. However, she suspected the teacher may have said something to incite the parent who was probably a volatile person herself. You can avoid such incidents by always being respectful to parents and always concentrating on the *work* done or not done, not the *child*. That is to say, a child is not "bad" but a child may submit "poor work." How you choose your words is very important. Because of this incident from her past, Ms. Valletta assigned two teachers to every room during conference days. There is safety in numbers.

The session ended with all agreeing to share their experiences from the upcoming parent conferences at the next workshop.

The next four sessions began with the usual discussion of questions raised by any of the workshop participants. And they did share their parent conference experiences. Once this segment was completed, each of the next four sessions was turned over to an assistant principal so he or she could speak to the participants about his or her duties and explain what help he or she could provide. Some of this had already been reviewed by the principal in previous sessions, either through planned parts of presentations or in response to questions raised.

However, the principal wanted her new staff to actually meet these assistant principals and wanted her assistant principals to personally meet any new staff members they had not yet encountered. The four assistant principals who conducted these sessions were the Assistant Principal (AP)/Pupil Personnel Services (i.e., student guidance), accompanied by a guidance counselor; the AP/Organization; the AP/Security, accompanied by one or more of the deans and a school security guard; and the AP/Instructional Support Services (special education). Every school is organized differently, and any principal seeking to establish a series of workshops for new teachers will call upon different personnel for such sessions.

After these presentations, workshop number thirteen dealt with the proctoring of the standardized examinations required by the state. During the January and June testing periods, regular classes were suspended so that there would be classroom space available for students to sit for exams and teacher time available to proctor and score them. At the end of the twelfth session, Ms. Valletta asked the new teachers to read the appropriate section of the *Teacher Handbook*. While district and state testing requirements are different, proctoring procedures tend to be standard (see textbox at the end of this chapter).

The principal answered questions about these procedures and stressed that the new teachers were responsible for fair administration of these exams. She noted that periodically, either the district or state would send auditors to the school to check that all regulations regarding exam security and proctoring were being followed.

Ms. Valletta had the group discuss their own experiences as students in high school taking standardized tests. It was amazing how many knew of students who had cheated. Occasionally one of the participants admitted to cheating, but only once. As time went by, Ms. Valletta updated this session to include instruction on how to proctor in an electronic age of cell phones and texting.

She related an anecdote from her own experiences. It was June near the end of her fifth year of teaching. Earlier in the day, at about 2 pm, the marking committee had completed the rating of the state examinations. One of her tasks, as assistant to the chairman, was to collate and then post these results on the department bulletin board so students could check their grades on this test, a graduation requirement. She had just completed this task at about 4 pm.

Students who had completed other exams were coming to check their grades. A student reported that she had taken the exam, but her name was not posted. Ms. Valletta told her not to worry. She would check the papers, already in alphabetical order. She did not find her exam. In the meantime, two more students reported the same problem. She caught the chair as he was leaving. They both knew something was wrong.

All these students had taken the exam in the same room, so they checked this room to determine if the exams had inadvertently been left in a desk drawer or closet. They found nothing. Then, they looked in the room exam envelope to be sure no papers had been left inside. None had been. Finally, they went through the detritus of the exam, all of which was kept, the scrap paper and question booklets. They found the students' answer papers stuffed inside their question booklets, even though the proctors had been clearly instructed to separate these booklets from the answer papers.

They found 10 exams. As the results of these exams determined graduation, both stayed late and marked them. Next June, proctors were not allowed to just turn in exam envelopes. They were asked to remove the answer papers in front of the collector and to sign a verification that the number of answer papers corresponded to the number of students who sat for the exam. There is a reason for every procedure.

Ms. Valletta also related an anecdote told to her by a colleague. Ms. Jill was principal of one of the "premier" schools in the city, where students vied for seats in Ivy League universities. The motive for cheating in such a school is not passing an exam, but maximizing the grade, making a 95, 99, or 100. Ms. Jill described how hall proctors became suspicious when students asking to leave the testing room to go to the bathroom all seemed to be going to the same bathroom, not necessarily the nearest one.

On inspecting the room when it was empty, the hall proctor found exam answers written on toilet paper. Thereafter, Ms. Jill's hall proctors periodically checked restrooms during exams to be sure no exchange of information was going on. The lesson for new teachers: There is no limit to the ingenuity of students intent on cheating. Always be on your guard.

In the final fall session, the principal tossed out the question "What will you do differently next semester?" This high school reorganized for the spring, so the teachers would have a new set of classes and students, giving them a chance to start over. The principal wanted to see if what had been discussed during these workshop sessions had had an impact. She had also personally observed each of these teachers two or three times and wanted to know if her suggestions and those of her assistant principals would be implemented.

Most of the responses dealt with how the teachers would handle discipline and especially how they would set up their classes the first day and the first weeks. Most also added how they would plan their marking procedures in advance so students would be aware of their responsibilities from the beginning of the class. Some wanted to improve their lesson planning and execution. Several spring workshop sessions would be devoted to lesson, unit, and semester planning.

Ms. Valletta ended with a comment on her own bias as a pedagogue: For most teachers, the keys to success are being fair to all, having a sense of humor, being well-organized, establishing and maintaining classroom routines, and being just a little bit unpredictable. They discussed how their plans for the new semester would incorporate these ideas. Then, there was a small party to celebrate the end of their first semester.

GUIDELINES FOR PROCTORING EXAMINATIONS

Preliminaries

- When the end of term bulletin is published, check your assignments (proctoring, reserve, marking, etc.). If you have any questions or problems, see the Assistant Principal of Organization in Room XXX immediately.
- Prior to picking up the exam, prepare your assigned room for a testing situation: separate desks, erase the board, and remove any posters or papers related to the test.
- Everything needed for the test is in the exam envelope. *Be sure you are wearing a watch that keeps accurate time.*

Before the Examination Begins

- Exam envelopes will be available for pick-up in Room XXX 15 minutes before the start of the exam. Please pick up your envelope as soon as it is available.
- The envelope will contain specific instructions for that particular exam. Read these instructions carefully.
- Seat the students as they arrive. Keep the rows nearest the entry door vacant so latecomers can be accommodated without disrupting students taking the test.
- Have students put all books and papers in a place that makes them inaccessible, such as the front of the room or the floor under their desks. They should have only pens, pencils, and erasers on their desks. For mathematics and science exams, check your instructions to see what other items are permissible.
- Arrange materials in the test envelope neatly on your desk to facilitate distribution.
- To get the test off to a quick start—many students need every minute of time—put two pieces of scrap paper on each desk; if the test uses a separate answer sheet (or Scantron form), put one on each desk. Write on the board that students are to make no marks on any paper until you direct them to.
- *Before* distributing the exam booklet, advise students to read the questions carefully and follow instructions; make sure their name and all other required information appears on each answer sheet; mark all machine-scored answer sheets in pencil; write all essays in pen using blue or black ink only; and use only a pencil for drawings and

(*continued*)

diagrams. Finally, remind students to sign the declaration printed on the answer booklet. [The declaration is a statement that the student did not cheat on the exam.]

During the Examination

- Have the students place their photo ID on the desk in front of them. As you give each student a question paper (face down), check that the face on the ID matches the face of the student. Students without an ID must be sent to Room XXX for identification verification. When all the papers have been distributed, have the students turn them over and begin to work.
- Follow the proctoring instructions. If you have any problems or questions, have the hall proctor contact the subject area supervisor in charge of the examination.
- You CANNOT help the student with the exam in any way. This means you CANNOT read or interpret any of the directions on the test or define any of the words used on the test. Students entitled to special testing considerations have been assigned to a separate testing room.
- The testing begins the second you tell the students to turn over their papers. Record this time on the board. If no clock is visible in the room, write on the board: TEST BEGAN: _____ TEST ENDS: _____ TIME NOW: _____. Change the TIME NOW every 15 minutes; when there are 30 minutes left, make a verbal announcement.
- Once the students have begun to work, take a post at the BACK of the room where you can see the students but they cannot see you. Every 15 minutes, circulate around the room (and change the TIME NOW on the board). As latecomers arrive, check their photo ID and have them begin the test. *They get no extra time.*
- As per State Education Department regulations, no student may leave the exam room until 10:15 (AM Test) or 2:15 (PM Test). No student may enter the exam room after 10:00 AM or 2:00 PM.
- *Proctoring is the active supervision of the room. It means looking at students continuously and taking responsibility for the integrity of the examination.* You cannot do this while reading a book, magazine or newspaper, marking exams, or seeing how much you know on the test you are proctoring.
- If you suspect cheating, make a written report of your suspicions. Ask the hall proctor to contact the subject supervisor in charge of the examination. Do not confront the student(s) yourself and create a disruptive situation in the exam room.

At the End of the Examination

- For the last 30 minutes of the examination, stand at the front of the room to facilitate the collection of papers. Arrange returned papers according to the instructions given. Student answer papers are batched separately from the question booklets.
- If a student hands in an exam early, you may say, "There are still XX minutes left. You may use this time to check your paper." You CANNOT give any specific advice, such as "You didn't answer essay 2—go back and do it."
- At the end of the three-hour examination period, collect the remaining papers. You cannot give anyone any extra time.
- Check that the number of answer papers you have collected corresponds to the number of students who were in your room.
- Put all materials in the exam envelope and bring the envelope to the room indicated in the proctoring instructions.

Chapter Seven

Training and Retaining New Teachers: The Spring Semester

Most of Ms. Valletta's spring semester workshops were devoted to methodology. The principal tried to help these almost-new teachers bridge the gap between the theory they had learned in the university and the reality of the classroom. All had classroom management strategies working to a satisfactory degree so they could concentrate on higher teaching skills. Developing such skills improves management even more, for nothing enhances discipline better than well-planned, motivating lessons.

An entire session was devoted to strategies for motivating instruction. Other sessions were devoted to planning lessons and units, varying instructional methods, honing one's questioning techniques, and preparing effective review lessons for both classroom and standardized tests. Strategies for handling major assignments, such as projects and term papers, were discussed. There was a workshop on the importance of students keeping good notebooks and suggestions for making homework assignments meaningful.

Many school leaders are well versed in instructional theory and methodology. If this describes you, skip the following discussion. Other school leaders move along a fast track and advance to leadership positions before becoming master teachers. If this describes you, you may want to read these pages that provide more details on motivating instruction and other aspects of pedagogy.

Ms. Valletta had briefly addressed motivational methods during the first workshop session in September. Other aspects were discussed during the open discussion parts of other workshops and in post-observation conferences. The various assistant principals also discussed this fine art of engaging students with their new teachers. This workshop that kicked off the spring semester was intended to bring all these strands together.

Ms. Valletta asked the participants to share some of the motivations they used in the fall semester. After each had spoken, she referred to their examples to categorize the motivations described.

- Using theatrics (as Ms. Valletta had seen an English teacher do in a lesson several years ago). Mr. Borg was teaching *Macbeth* to an average junior class. As he explained in the post-observation conference, he believed *Macbeth* was the perfect play to teach students about Shakespeare and his audience. It had witches, spells, a strong if crazy female character, sleepwalking, murder, mayhem, and double talk.

  The day he brought the texts to distribute seemed normal. The board had the aim and the homework indicated. Mr. Borg was at the door greeting students as they arrived. No one noticed he had pulled down all the shades on the windows. When everyone was seated, he ambled over to the light switch and, just as he shut off all the lights, let out a cackle to curdle one's blood. Students jumped out of their seats as he began reading the first lines from the play, using a flashlight to light up his contorted face. This bit of theatrics got the attention of his juniors and unsuspecting observing principal.

  He built on this motivation to explain how Shakespeare's audience reacted to seeing witches on stage—exactly as the students did when he cackled. This led into the world of Elizabethan theater and the themes of *Macbeth* so well summarized in the opening lines of the play. After distributing the text, Mr. Borg continued to dramatically read from the play, helping students see how reading aloud made the language easier to understand. He had hooked his students on reading and enjoying Shakespeare.
- Relating the topic of the lesson to the students' lives and interests or current events. A biology lesson Ms. Valletta observed a few years previously featured a motivating discussion on cloning, shortly after the Dolly the sheep story hit the media. The students were engrossed in the discussion, a lead-in to a lesson on DNA.
- Involving students in an ethical dilemma. The teacher tries to place students in a "real situation." The day before Ms. Miller began teaching *The Crucible*, she gave a short vocabulary quiz. Midway through the quiz, a colleague called her out of the room. Ms. Valletta, a part of the deception, walked by and looked through the classroom window. Ms. Miller returned in five minutes, collected the papers, and taught the day's lesson.

The next day she came into the classroom looking distracted. She uncharacteristically stammered as she explained:

> I don't like doing this, but my job here is on the line if I don't. Yesterday, while I was out of the room, the principal passed by and looked in—some of you may have seen her (affirmative nods from a few students). She saw some of you cheating on the quiz. She took down the seat locations of those she saw. Ms. Valletta was angry that so many of you could be so dishonest and blamed me for not teaching you to know better. (At this point, Ms. Miller gave each student a sheet of paper.) On this piece of paper, please write your name. If you cheated yesterday, write down "Yes, I cheated." The principal said that she would have the deans go easy on those who confessed. Next, please write the name of anyone else you know was cheating (grumbles from the class). I know—no one wants to rat on a classmate, but she knows anyway. If you are honest, it will go easier on all of us.

Ms. Miller collected the papers and put them in a folder. She then asked the class how doing this made them feel. She assured them they could be honest. And so began a discussion on the main theme of *The Crucible*, which they better understood having gone through this McCarthyist exercise. She destroyed the papers in front of the class.

- Revealing strange biographical information about a personage to be mentioned in the lesson. Ben Franklin seems dull to most students, but talk about his early morning streaking through the streets of Boston or his various romantic indiscretions, real and rumored, and he becomes human and interesting. Then there's Dante Gabriel Rossetti's disinterment of his wife to get back the only copy of his poems which he buried with her in a fit of grief. Let's not forget the Archimedes "Eureka" story. Fortunately, many of the great people in all fields were a bit crazy—even Shakespeare left his wife "the second best bed." Biographical anecdotes can enliven the lesson.
- Helping students visualize mathematical and geometrical concepts. Ms. Valletta's math/science chair believed in helping make manipulatives available to his teachers. He made sure science teachers had many colorful models of the heart, brain, digestive system, etc. As Ms. Valletta observed his teachers, she could see how these models motivated instruction by helping students visualize concepts.
- Adding to the aura of mystery surrounding the teacher's personal life. When teachers tell real or imaginary stories about their own lives, they get

their students' immediate attention. Ms. Valletta taught with Mr. Christie several decades ago. He used this story in his class:

> I was dating this girl who had a very strange sense of humor. One day, she and her friend decided to help the audience of a horror movie experience catharsis. (Mr. Christie, "What's catharsis?" "Mary, that's what we'll be talking about later—let's get back to my girlfriend"). This was an especially gory horror movie and near the end, blood was spouting out of hacked bodies. The manager of the theater had also added another element, having one of his ushers dress up as the maniacal killer and run through the center aisle wielding a bloody ax (it was rubber) during the climactic scene. The audience was already disgusted by the gore and then scared out of their wits when this fake fiend ran down the aisle.
>
> Now my girlfriend and her friend had a seat in the first row of the balcony. They brought a thermos filled with a mixture of warm oatmeal and melted cheese. At the climactic moment, when the blood was spouting and the maniac running down the aisle, they loudly made believe they were vomiting and poured their oatmeal concoction down on the unsuspecting audience below. Why did they do this? Their English teacher had just taught them about catharsis and they wanted to show this audience what it meant.

And, so began the lesson on the concept of catharsis in *Oedipus Rex*. He cautioned his students not to duplicate this stunt. The girls' parents had to pay the theater for seat cleaning and several patrons' dry-cleaning bills.

- Changing the arrangement of the students' desks before students arrive. This could signal a workshop session, debate, or other special type of lesson.
- Using a quiz show format for review sessions.
- Using a poem or short nonfiction piece to introduce the subject of lesson. The discussion of a lesson-related quotation or proverb can also motivate a lesson.

Ms. Valletta explained that when she started teaching, the developmental lesson, which always began with a motivation relating the lesson to the students' lives, was the be all and end all of instruction in New York City. After Ms. Valletta had done this for much of a semester, one student raised her hand and said, "Okay, we get it—cut to the chase and get on with the real lesson." Vary what you do each day so the students never know what treat to expect.

Many teachers begin a lesson with a good motivation, but forget to continue to motivate instruction throughout the lesson. There are several ways to do this.

- Referring back to the opening motivation when appropriate. Continue to use what worked. End the lesson with the summary question: How did the opening of this lesson help you better understand what was taught?
- Using humor. In essence, each teacher needs to develop his or her own shtick or persona. When Ms. Valletta saw a class getting antsy, she would turn around, talk to the chalkboard, and bang her head against it. The students knew this meant it was time to get back on task—and it was far more effective than raising her voice. She added that everyone present probably recalls one or more teachers who had such a shtick. She remembered many of her teachers on all levels, those we would call "characters."

  Unfortunately, in our world of political correctness and pre-canned instruction, we are in danger of losing such eccentrics who make education such a joy and help students learn about the variety of people they will encounter in the real world. She advised her new teachers: Be a character! They are welcome in the classroom as well as on the USA Network.
- Using visuals, computers, examples, modeling, acting. Ms. Valletta described how she saw a social studies teacher divide his class into the negotiators from different countries rearranging the map of Europe at the Congress of Vienna. Each group knew what it wanted and what it would settle for. The final map was not quite what really happened, but the students understood the process—and how the victors made sure the losers were punished.
- Appealing to as many senses as possible during every lesson. Sight and hearing are easy but does a lesson appeal to touch, taste, and smell? Multisensory instruction works very well in the elementary classroom. It is very effective in foreign language instruction. When teaching the words for the different fruits, a teacher can bring in as many fruits as possible so the students touch, smell, and, if they want, taste the lesson.
- Incorporating different types of activities. The best lessons include reading, writing, speaking, and listening.
- Really listening and responding to students. As a supervisor observing lessons, Ms. Valletta was amazed by how often teachers did not listen to student questions or responses. As a result, they often accepted poor responses or answered questions with non sequiturs.

- Putting student responses on the board—in the students' own words.
- Talking less. The more the students respond and the less the teacher talks, the better the lesson. In today's jargon, the teacher is the coach on the side, not the sage on the stage. A teacher does this by asking well-phrased, well-planned pivotal questions.

Finally, after motivating the lesson and continuing to use motivational methods throughout, the teacher should motivate the homework to encourage as many students as possible to complete the assignment:

- Always fully explain the homework and ask if there are any questions.
- If time permits, have students begin the homework in class as you circulate. Homework begun is more likely to be homework completed.
- Avoid rote assignments: Be creative!
- Have a class policy that homework attempted will always receive a minimum passing grade, but not doing homework earns a 0.

Lesson planning is covered in teacher preparation programs, traditional and alternative. Ms. Valletta's assistant principals discussed lesson planning with their new teachers throughout the fall semester. This second spring session was designed to have her new teachers evaluate and reflect upon their own lessons. She wanted them to consider eight questions regarding each lesson they planned and taught:

1. Why are you teaching this lesson? By answering this question, the teachers could seek ways to make the lesson relevant to their students, helping them understand why they needed to learn what was taught.
2. Did the lesson have a measurable learning objective? This is an era of data-driven instruction. Lesson outcomes need to be measurable. It is not acceptable for a teacher to want students to understand the causes of the Civil War. They must be able to write an essay in which they fully explain a minimum of three causes of the war.
3. Was there an opening activity, such as a do-now? The first few minutes of a class period are crucial. Students need to enter the room, take their seats, and begin working immediately. The teacher establishes routines and makes sure that instruction begins at the bell.
4. Was there a motivation? This relates to numbers one and three above and the motivation workshop.

5. Did the lesson plan have a sequential list of student activities and pivotal, thought-provoking questions?
6. Were these activities and questions relevant to the learning objective?
7. Did you include a summary activity to determine if the learning objective had been met? (This could be a homework assignment.)
8. Did the lesson plan have an "elastic ending"? This is not usually found in the standard texts and was based on Ms. Valletta's observation that one of the most difficult skills for a new teacher to learn is timing. A lesson that ran over could be completed the next day. A lesson that ran short left the new teacher standing in front of the room with nothing to do. The elastic ending was an extra activity or question that could serve as a filler if time was left. This could be a feedback quiz in which students are asked to describe, in writing, what they had learned during the lesson, hence fulfilling the requirement of a summary activity.

Ensuing workshops centered on long-term planning: for the week, for the unit, for the semester. The principal shared the planning calendar she had used as a teacher. Over the summer vacation and winter recess, she planned out her units and lessons for the coming semester. The longer she taught, the easier this became. After several years, there was no course she had not taught, so she had materials available for whatever program she was assigned.

She advised: Save everything. At the end of each day, reflect on what worked and what didn't and add this reflection to the lesson plan so the next time the lesson plan is used, adjustments can be made. The principal was amazed at how many teachers—even experienced ones—felt they had to write new plans every year, even when teaching a unit they had previously taught. The personality of each class is different, but as teachers gain experience, the same successful plan can be adapted and differentiated for the students in each class without rewriting it. The organized teacher should find that his or her job becomes easier every year.

Today's neophyte teacher will, in all probability, be dating, getting married, having children, and taking on parental and familial responsibilities. Unless the professional part of their lives can be appropriately limited, their personal lives will suffer. Good teachers find a balance between their personal and professional lives. A teacher without a personal life will be the poorer because there will be fewer personal experiences, less reading, and less travel to enrich their instruction. Many years ago, the principal recalled reading a survey conducted by the National Council of Teachers of English that revealed that English teachers read fewer than five books a year for their own personal reading pleasure. What a sad state of affairs! And we wonder why our students don't read.

After many years as a principal, Ms. Valletta added a session based on an all-day workshop that the district had provided principals. This was run by Rob Bocchino, Heart of Change, and dealt with better ways to involve students in instruction. It is rare that there is anything new under the sun in teaching; however, Mr. Bocchino packaged learning theory and practice in a new and accessible teacher-friendly manner. Ms. Valletta took some of his ideas and conveyed them to both her new teachers and some experienced staff members. As these materials are copyrighted, Google Heart of Change and its package "Essential Elements of Instruction" for more information.

There were four sessions that did not fall under the heading of instructional methods: "Planning School Trips," "The Uniqueness of the School," "Career Pathways and Planning for Your Future," and, the final session, "Feedback, Reflection, and Suggestions." The details of each follow.

"Planning School Trips." As her school was located in the heart of Manhattan, Ms. Valletta's students often went on school trips. Groups allied with the theater district often provided tickets for students both during and after the school day. Field trips to museums, business venues, and historical sites were common. Many were within walking distance of the school. The district was schizophrenic about school trips. On the one hand, a district bureaucrat would send a memo about how the city itself was a school and students should be exposed to its fine institutions. On the other hand, the paperwork required for any field trip, even one requiring only a short walk from the school, was immense. Part of this was healthy paranoia. If anything happened to a student while on a school-sanctioned trip, the district would bear part of the legal responsibility.

A chapter of the school's *Teacher Handbook* was devoted to planning a school trip. This workshop was devoted to reviewing this chapter with the new teachers to stress that all procedures had to be followed to prevent any liability on their part and on the part of the school administrator who approved the trip: the principal. Every district has its own procedures, designed to protect students and staff when they leave the building. Most will probably be similar to those described below.

To begin the session, the now not-so-new teachers brainstormed about school trips relevant to their subject areas. To be approved, all trips during regular school hours had to be educational in nature. Ms. Valletta explained how they would go about planning the trip.

First, she stressed that when teachers organize and chaperone a trip, they are taking *personal responsibility* for the health and safety of their students. They need to insure that all students are present and accounted for when they leave the school and when they arrive at the site. If any child is missing, the teacher had to contact the school and the police. If they were bringing students back to school after the trip, they could not leave the site until all students were present for the return. If there was a problem, they had to contact the school immediately.

Next, the principal discussed the application process for an approved trip. Teachers began by seeing her secretary, who would guide them through the procedures. Her secretary would give them a copy of the latest version of district regulations governing procedures for school trips as well as recent addenda. They would be asked to sign a statement that they would read these materials and follow the guidelines given. She would give the trip planners four forms for completion:

- Application for a School Trip (district form)
- Teacher Permission Form for a School Trip (school form)
- Parent Consent Form for Trips during the School Day (district form)
- Meetings/Trips outside the School Building (school form)

The "Application for a School Trip" had to be completed at least three weeks prior to the date of the planned trip. The form then had to be initialed by the department supervisor, signed by the principal, and forwarded to the district for final approval. If the form was not completed correctly or if the nature of the trip was not related to the educational program, it would *not* be approved.

Part of the application required that the teacher planning the trip verify there would be at least 1 adult chaperone for every 15 students. A licensed teacher had to be one of these adults. Parents of students could volunteer to be chaperones. Students' older siblings or significant others could *not* be chaperones. The principal advised teachers planning to use parent chaperones to begin with a student-chaperone ratio of 10:1 so that chaperone no-shows would not force a trip cancellation. (District regulations specified lower required student-chaperone ratios for middle and elementary schools.)

For overnight trips, special forms, permissions, and insurance were needed. All overnight trips had to be planned in conjunction with the student activities advisor and the AP/Security. The time frame for approval was six weeks for overnight trips. Such trips were rare. The school had an annual senior trip over the mid-winter recess (since no instructional time was lost, this trip did not have to be educational in nature). The College Counselor also planned trips to different university campuses.

The "Teacher Permission Form for a School Trip" was used when students would miss other classes in order to go on a trip during the school day. Because the school had so many trips, some teachers were concerned about students missing lessons, especially students not doing well in their classes. A school policy addressed this issue: Students are not automatically excused from classes to go on a trip. They must obtain permission from the teachers whose classes they will miss. To qualify for the *privilege* of going on a school trip, a student must be passing the class and have satisfactory attendance. There were time frames for the student to obtain the necessary signatures and return the forms to the trip planners.

The parent of each child going on the trip had to complete the "Parent Consent Form for Trips during the School Day." The teachers in charge would fill in all the information on the trip so parents would be aware of where their children were going and how they would travel to and from the location. Then, they would duplicate this form and give a copy to each child at least two weeks prior to the trip date. A parent had to complete the form and give it to the child to return at least two days prior to the day of the trip. In addition to indicating permission, the parent had to give daytime contact numbers and information on any health issues or medications relating to the child. The teachers would carry these forms on the trip.

When she led trips for her department as an assistant principal, Ms. Valletta often had her sister, a registered nurse, along as a chaperone. Luckily, no student ever had a health problem on any of these trips.

When Ms. Valletta's sister chaperoned a trip for her own child's school, however, the importance of having parent consent forms along was made very real. The elementary school was on a non-school day field trip to an amusement park. When he got off the bus, a student informed his teacher that he had forgotten his medication. Ms. Valletta's sister was called in. It turned out the student had had a heart transplant and forgotten his anti-rejection medicine. Using the information on the parent form, she contacted the mother who in turn gave her the name of the child's cardiologist. He advised that the child could take the medication when he returned home.

The "Meetings/Trips outside the School Building" form was a simple half-page paper used whenever any staff member, including the principal, would be out of the building for all or part of a school day. In the days before the proliferation of cell phones, it provided emergency contact information.

When the principal completed describing all these procedures and providing the teachers with blank forms, many simply shook their heads and said it was not worth it. In many ways she agreed. She advised them not to plan any trip alone, but to work in conjunction with an experienced teacher. Despite the administrative obstacles, school trips added new dimensions to the education their students.

"The Uniqueness of the School." Every school is unique in its own way. Ms. Valletta was proud of her school's music and theater programs. A highlight of the school year was an annual evening spring musicale usually held the third Friday and Saturday in May.

Students in the theater program, under the supervision of their teachers, obtained the necessary copyright releases. They planned publicity, lighting, staging, scenery, and props. Teachers in the theater program collaborated with teachers and students in the music department. While students in the theater program were given special consideration, all students in the school could audition for parts in the spring production, usually a musical comedy. As the show approached and rehearsals became more and more necessary, some students were excused from classes. Over time, Ms. Valletta directed staff to minimize this by scheduling rehearsals during the theater and music classes themselves, during lunch periods, and after the end of the last class.

This particular workshop session was held in the midst of the spring musicale frenzy, shortly before the scheduled performances. Some teachers were concerned by their students' obsession with the show. Others were upset because, despite the school's efforts, some students were missing their classes for rehearsals.

Ms. Valletta addressed these issues by first reviewing the history of the school. When the school opened in the 1950's, the principal sought a way to make the school unique. In an era prior to the stress on academic testing, he wanted to find a way for all students, even those not academically gifted, to display their talents. A fan of Rodgers and Hammerstein, he made sure he funded a band/choral program and specialized classes in theater. A class in each program was required to meet the state requirement for a music and art class. Students could elect to continue with advanced classes, programs permitting. They demonstrated their talents in a spring musicale, which became a tradition that future principals continued.

Even when the dual pressures of budget cuts and more standardized testing made it difficult, Ms. Valletta felt it important to maintain these programs (with some trimming) because they provided a non-academic venue where students could shine. She brought yearbooks dating back to the founding of the school so the workshop participants could see a progression of spring musicale presentations and costumes over the decades.

The theater and music programs and spring musicale helped make Manhattan High different from other district schools. They were integral parts of the school's identity. Since the 1980's, students from outside the school's designated feeder district could apply to these specialized programs, increasing the school's population and providing some of these new teachers with their jobs.

At this point Ms. Valletta digressed, relating some of the lore of the school—stories handed down through generations of teachers. Part of the ambience of a school is its lore. It is important for the older generation to pass these stories down to the younger. There was the story of the founding principal who had a china and silver service for himself. His table in the cafeteria was always set for him and his lunch brought to him. No one could approach unless summoned. Ah, the good old days of autocratic principals!

And, of course, there was the inevitable story of the administrator caught *in flagrante delicto* with a female staff member (in those days of yore before women's liberation or awareness of sexual harassment). There were more stories, some involving current staff members. She told these so that the legends would continue and often wondered if she would someday be the subject of such legends.

After this diversion into the myths of the school, Ms. Valletta discussed how to handle instruction during the two-week period prior to the musicale. As June testing would soon be approaching, it was a good time to review; in classes not ending in an exam, nonsequential creative lessons would be appropriate. She ended by giving the teachers free passes to the Friday performance of the show. Of course, she hoped they would bring along significant others, parents, friends, etc., who would have to pay for their tickets. Monies raised were used to cover the expenses of the special programs, such as instruments, materials for scenery, and props and costumes.

In academic classrooms, teachers see only one side of their students. Many students in every school are not verbal or mathematical learners. They display other intelligences: visual/spatial, musical/rhythmic, interpersonal. At this show, academic teachers could see that a child struggling with math or science or social studies or English, might be a first-rate musician or set designer or singer or actor. In schools lacking such unique programs, academic teachers might never see this side of their students and never understand that every child has the talent to shine in one way or another. The feedback Ms. Valletta received from the new teachers who attended the show was always the same: They were amazed by the talents of their students.

At this session, Ms. Valletta also advised her new teachers to attend at least one varsity basketball, volleyball, or baseball game to see their students excel in yet another type of intelligence.

All schools have some major event; some schools have several. It is important for school leaders to stress that every student has talents a school should foster. School leaders need to highlight the uniqueness, the history and lore, and the special programs of their schools to their new staff members who will add to this uniqueness, history, and lore and maybe even begin a new program wherein students may shine.

"Career Pathways and Planning for Your Future." In early June, as the school year drew to a close, the principal wanted her new teachers to think about their futures. The first six or so times Ms. Valletta conducted this session, it was called "Career Pathways." She wanted her first-year teachers to think about their lives several years in the future.

Did they want to be the master teachers in their departments? Did they want to go into educational leadership? Were they more interested in helping students one-on-one and did they therefore feel counseling or social work might be in their future? How could the skills they developed as teachers be used in professions outside this school? Perhaps, they would want to teach at the college or university level. Perhaps they wanted to leave public education entirely and enter the private sector in a managerial position. The principal went over these different options and provided as much information as she could on each. She always stressed that they would never find as much job satisfaction in jobs outside of the school.

Ms. Valletta wanted to convince these teachers to remain in her school. In later years, she added information on the short- and long-term benefits of remaining a teacher or administrator in the school district and state. Every school system is different. However, in general, the public sector usually provides better benefits than the private sector to compensate for generally lower salaries. It is important for school leaders to learn about these benefits and explain them to their new teachers to encourage them to remain with the school.

This is vital in an age when young people enter the workforce with the idea that they will be changing jobs several times during their lifetime. The concept of staying with the same organization for one's entire career is viewed as quaint, at best. But, this is just what a school leader wants to sell to new teachers. The school's leadership staff and master teachers have devoted hundreds of hours to helping these teachers become competent and then master teachers to serve the children of the school and district. If they leave for greener pastures in other school systems or the private sector, this time is wasted, continuity of staff is reduced, and new teachers must be hired and trained.

Ms. Valletta fully explained the benefits of remaining with the school and district. These included:

- Excellent medical coverage for themselves, their significant other, and children.
- Additional dental and vision coverage provided through the union.
- A strong pension plan which, at the time, allowed a teacher with 30 years of experience to retire at age 55 with a take-home pension that exceeded his or her final year's salary. By law, the pension was exempt from state and local income taxes. An option allowed a teacher to cover a surviving spouse or significant other.
- An optional tax-deferred annuity program. Teachers could have a certain percentage of their salary deducted for investment in a variety of alternatives: a traditional interest-bearing account (with a minimum interest rate legislated at 7 percent), a mutual fund with a variety of options, or a less-volatile bond mutual fund. Money contributed would be tax-deferred, reducing their current federal, state, and local income taxes. Wise investments in this program meant that many teachers retired with hundreds of thousands of dollars.
- A generous sick and personal day allowance. Teachers were given 10 per year. Days not used accumulated in a "sick bank" which could then be used to provide full salary during a major illness. Up to 200 days could be accumulated. Days not used at retirement would be redeemed for a cash payment at the rate of one day's pay for every two days in the bank. Ms.

Valletta explained that this was much better than it sounded. Days saved at the new teacher's current rate of pay would be worth double or even triple at retirement, so even at two for one, teachers were coming out ahead.
- As long as the teacher remained within the district in any capacity—teacher, assistant principal, principal, district administrator, etc.—all benefits were transferable. Most were also transferable to positions within the municipal university system and educational positions elsewhere in the state.

She concluded with the most important part of this workshop: All these benefits will guarantee these new teachers comfortable lives and secure retirements. They will not get as rich as most accountants, lawyers, stock brokers, real estate agents, or corporate executives. But they will change lives. They will not always know this, but they can be sure that every year they will positively impact the lives of children. Some children will decide not to drop out because of them. Some will become the first in their family to attend college. Some, born into poverty, will enter middle-class lives, affecting their families for generations to come.

The good these teachers do with their lives as educators can never be measured in dollars and cents and will be far more satisfying than balancing accounts, arguing legal points, selling stocks or real estate, or managing a corporation for profit. Their lives will be measured by the inestimable good they do for children.

"Feedback, Reflection, and Suggestions." The final session in mid-June was a debriefing for the year. The principal provided refreshments and asked the participants in the New Teacher Workshops to share their reflections on their first year of teaching. These included how they saw their growth as professionals, their candid evaluation of the value of the workshops, their views on the staff development they had been given by the principal and their supervising assistant principals. No subject was off-limits.

Ms. Valletta ended this session by asking her new teachers a favor: To always give her and their other supervisors the benefit of the doubt. As they continued as teachers, they might look at some decisions and actions taken by the leadership staff and think them unexplainable or even stupid. When that happened, the principal asked these teachers to come to see her first so that she could try to explain the situation and, if necessary, remedy it.

An underlying purpose of these sessions and her own intensive one-on-one work with new teachers through the observation process was to build their loyalty to the school as a whole and to her personally. Loyalty is an important attribute of a staff member. A principal needs staff support, especially in times of crisis. Such loyalty makes it possible for a principal to move a school forward. Ms. Valletta was trying to build this loyalty from the ground up by having new staff members see her as an instructional leader whose main goals were having them succeed as teachers and having their students reach their potentials. In the ensuing years, she wanted them to trust her so that they could bring any issue to her for resolution, not to the union and its cumbersome grievance process.

Educational leaders resemble politicians. They need to build a cadre of loyal followers. Assistant principals and chairpersons develop this loyalty by being fair and providing support for the instruction provided by their teachers. Principals, especially in larger schools, need to reach out to new staff and personally work with them. They need to build trust one-on-one during their encounters with individual teachers. They can build this loyalty with new staff through the workshops just described. Even in schools with low teacher turnover, principals who serve for 10 or more years will find that they have hired and trained the majority of the staff in the school by the end of their tenures.

Another way to retain good staff, both new and experienced, is to make sure they have a pleasant work environment. Hence it is important to develop and nurture a positive school ambience, the next pillar of successful school leadership.

Chapter Eight

Creating a Positive School Ambience: Respect, Instruction, Welcome

Students and staff spend the better part of their days in school. Teachers are there at least eight hours. For school leaders, this increases to 10 on most days. Students have a regular school day of six to seven hours, but a large percentage will arrive early or stay late for school-related activities. Unlike in the private sector, a school cannot offer gourmet cafeteria food or relaxation rooms or swimming pools (well, schools with pools might be able to do this) or state-of-the-art building amenities and technology.

School leaders must rely on themselves to make their institutions good places to learn and teach. A school may have low student achievement with a positive ambience, but it cannot have high student achievement without a positive ambience. This positive ambience is a basic building block for student achievement and staff morale and continuity.

The first three components of a plan to improve school ambience are Respect and Understanding; Instructional Components; and How the School Welcomes New Students.

1. *Respect and Understanding*

An ambience of respect and understanding must pervade the school. The way a principal treats the staff will be mirrored by the way the staff treats students, parents, and each other. If teachers observe school leaders treating students, parents, and staff with kindness and respect, they will emulate this. Second to the hiring and training of new teachers, this is how the principal and leadership team create a workplace of mutual and sincere respect and understanding.

It is not easy. Spending the better part of one's day teaching students is the most difficult of jobs. Any parent who has ever lost it when dealing with one or two children can understand how a teacher may have one of those days when dealing with a multitude of children. School leaders, addressing people issues every day, must guard against the human tendency to drop the mask of the serene school leader and just let it all out. We can all become frustrated by the foibles and inanity of our colleagues, our students, and our students' parents. But, they and we are human and therefore innately imperfect.

When the staff sees the principal and assistant principals stay calm in all situations, they are more likely to stay calm themselves. Students emulate the adults around them. If these adults treat one another and students with respect, the students, as far as they are able, will return this respect. Students will do so "as far as they are able" because students are not fully formed people. Even high school students are still adults-in-process, dealing with peer pressures and the middle years of puberty. When students act out, adults must respond as adults with an understanding of the physical, emotional, and social turmoil of childhood, pre-adolescence, and adolescence.

As teachers, we enjoy working with children, but children, especially preteens and teenagers, like to test the system, whether by trying to see how far they can go with a new teacher, sneaking a ride on the teacher elevator, or pushing the limits of acceptable dress. If we understand this, we can deal with them. If we forget this, we lose it.

In today's world, it is difficult to see children as children. Our society has been taking away childhood piece by piece, as we want our children to be constantly excelling in school, music, dance, soccer, hockey, or whatever. Even the little ones leave school only to move on to another activity and then home to mounds of homework. Instead of free play time to use their imaginations, children have play groups, play dates, and Internet interactions. Is it any wonder that by the middle school years, these children have a veneer of sophistication as they seek to emulate the role models media puts before them—American idols and Hollywood "stars" with their suggestive dress, questionable lifestyles, and illicit shenanigans? We sometimes treat our students as adults because of this veneer, but we must remember that under it all, they are still children. As their adult role models, we need to provide them with positive mores.

We do much of this instructionally, the next component for creating a positive school ambience.

2. Instructional Components

This topic has two aspects: ethical education and motivational teaching.

It is an unwritten (or in some school systems, perhaps written) law of public education never to teach a formalized set of moral or ethical values. Teachers, in positions of authority, must never even implicitly impose their own personal beliefs as this would violate separation of church and state. This has led the religious right to accuse public schools of teaching the godless morality of secular humanism, and it becomes an argument for giving children a private, narrowly religious education either in autonomous charter schools or church-sponsored schools or through home-schooling.

All good teachers teach ethics and morals—and not secular humanism—because a major goal of public education is to provide the country with good citizens, workers, and parents. Ethics and morality pervade our national documents, such as the Declaration of Independence and the Constitution, framed, despite references to God, by men who were for the most part atheists, agnostics, secular humanists, or believers in an impersonal deity.

Principal Thelen's background as an English teacher influenced his thinking on this issue, for how does one teach great literature (or even teenage and kiddie lit) without grappling with moral issues? How does one approach *The Scarlet Letter* without having students probe the morality of its different characters? How does one teach *Macbeth* without looking at evil in the world?

Mr. Thelen remembers a particular lesson he taught on Act IV of *Othello*. In Scene iii, a distraught Desdemona, just accused by her jealous husband of being unfaithful, asks her maid, Emilia, if "there be women do abuse their husbands/In such gross kind?" Emilia responds, "There be some such, no question." Desdemona asks the question, "Wouldst thou do such a deed for all the world?" Emilia responds, "The world's a huge thing. It is a great price for a small vice."

His motivation for this lesson, taught many times from the early 1970's through the late 1980's, was to pose this moral issue to the class:

- Gentlemen, you are on your honeymoon with your beautiful wife. A stranger, taken by her beauty, offers you one million dollars to let him sleep with her. Would you take it? (Yes, this later became a movie with Robert Redford. Mr. Thelen wonders if someone in his class back in the 70's worked on the screenplay.)

- Ladies, you are on your honeymoon with your new husband. A stranger offers you one million dollars to let her sleep with him—and your husband would never know. Would you do it?

Mr. Thelen never imposed his own morality on these questions, but permitted the students to freely discuss the issue and, in doing so, to develop their own moral barometers so they could better understand the characters of Desdemona, the idealist, and Emilia, the more morally ambiguous realist in the play. *Othello* was part of the curriculum. Could it be taught without addressing these moral issues and ambiguities? Without having students look at their own values as they impact their understanding of the characters?

Over the many years he taught this lesson, there was a distinct change in the attitudes of his students. At all times, most students were adamant that they would refuse—that love was more important than money. However, in the early 1970's, several boys would take the offer while no girls would. By the mid-1980's this was reversed. He wonders if this was an unanticipated consequence of boys finding their feminine sides and girls being liberated.

Teachers should be encouraged to challenge their students to think ethically about the issues raised by the curriculum in all subject areas. As previously noted, shortly after the Dolly the sheep story made headlines, Principal Valletta observed a biology teacher begin a lesson on cell structure by asking students if they thought cloning was ethical. During the discussion, the students in the class gave fine responses touching on a spectrum of opinions on this issue. Today, a teacher could ask a similar question about stem cell research.

Ethics must also be addressed in the teaching of social studies, whether in looking at the policies of world leaders, the decisions of the Supreme Court or the use (or abuse) of natural resources by first world nations. The now quaint word *citizenship* and what it means falls under the auspices of social studies instruction.

In his academic-vocational school, Mr. Thelen had an extra advantage in providing students with an ethical education: his occupational teachers incorporated the ethics of the workplace into their instruction. In the workplace, one treats all coworkers and customers with fairness and respect; one is not prejudiced toward others for any reason; one is respectful of authority; one cares about the appearance of oneself and one's work space. This type of instruction fulfills a school's major responsibility: To train the future workers of our country.

Knowing this, had Mr. Thelen become the principal of a non-vocational school, he would have sought to incorporate these values into the curriculum. This ethical approach was supported by his many speakers from the business community who addressed students on how they achieved success and the expectations business managers had for their employees.

The first way we improve school ambience through instruction is by having students understand ethical implications and develop their own ethical sense. The second way is by providing students with motivating, well-planned instruction. A positive school ambience is established when students know that each of their teachers will begin teaching from the beginning of the period, will make instruction interesting to them, will explain concepts in ways that can be understood, will respond to their questions with patience, and will, ultimately, evaluate their work fairly.

Students motivated by good teaching arrive on time and are attentive in class. They are not cutting class, roaming the hallways, or being referred to the deans. Students genuinely engaged by instruction do not ask for passes or disrupt the class. Good instruction enhances a school's ambience. A major responsibility of school leaders is the training of teachers so that they provide just such instruction, as described in the previous three chapters.

3. *How the School Welcomes New Students*

The third component of a school ambience plan is how the school welcomes its new students. This applies equally on all levels of instruction, though the methodology is different.

In the elementary school, the new students are usually five-year-old kindergarten children. As mandatory pre-K instruction becomes more widespread, these children will begin school at an even earlier age. In districts with extreme poverty, whether urban or rural, many children have not been to school previously for more than a few hours a week, if at all. They have not had to meet the demands of being in class with twenty or more other children and meeting pre-set achievement goals. The kindergarten (or pre-K) teacher has, perhaps, the most important responsibility in all education: To make this first year of schooling one in which children come to value learning, develop their imaginations, and learn the fundamentals of good living. American author Robert Fulghum had it right—all one needs to know about life *is* learned in kindergarten.

School leaders must try to insure that the first teachers children encounter are the very best they can find. They need to insure that these teachers understand their critical role in helping children begin their lives as students—lives that will continue through grade 12 and, ideally, through college and then into their adult lives as life-long learners.

School leaders must also have special programs for the parents of incoming students so these parents understand their new role as they send their children off to school. The parents need to know what they can expect from their children, from the teachers, and from the school. They need to understand how their roles as parents will change. In the best of all possible circumstances, there should be workshops for these parents so they can learn the basics of the instruction that will be provided to their children and be prepared to help them at home in ways that support the instruction of the school. More than at any other level, every effort must be made to make these parents regular partners with the school and frequent attendees of meetings and workshops.

In most districts, middle school includes grades six, seven, and eight, although there are variations on this. In rural and many suburban districts, the transition to middle school is not as severe as in large urban districts. In these smaller venues, the middle school is an extension of the elementary school, often in the same building or on the same campus. There is no trauma of movement to a new location or getting used to new classmates. There is a change in instructional methodology, going from a classroom with one teacher (with some cluster instruction) to subject area instruction.

The same pedagogical issue exists in large urban districts, but in addition, students usually find themselves in a totally new location with different school rules and regulations, with different classmates in the school as a whole and in each class in particular. As several elementary schools feed into one middle school, the new institution is significantly larger than the one the student was used to. And, for all schools, students formerly at the top of the heap in grade five now fall to the bottom in grade six.

Tweens face the physical, emotional, and psychological issues of preadolescence. The school leaders of the middle school need to plan a welcome program to help these students adjust to their new environment, the more rigorous curriculum (and testing), and the new instructional methods. This should involve a welcome orientation for students and parents, special orientation materials incorporated into the instruction of the first few weeks, and a program designed to help these students succeed in their first year in middle school. All of these strategies are discussed below in relation to the first year of high school. Middle school leaders can adapt them to the sixth grade.

Mr. Thelen's experiences creating a program to welcome new students to his academic-vocational school are relevant to this discussion. When he became principal mid-year, he inherited the initial stages of a grant program sponsored by a charitable foundation interested in his school's occupational program. He took his predecessor's place on the planning committee to determine how this foundation could best support the students of the school. As part of the data review, he noticed some startling numbers. Each year, the school began with about 400 ninth year students. Four years later, the June graduating class was about 200.

Two hundred students did not drop out. Most were still juniors or sophomores or even freshmen, based on their credit accumulation. The members of the committee looked at the 200 students who made it to the senior year on time. Invariably, these students had passed all their classes in the ninth year. Students still classified as juniors had failed two or even three ninth year classes and many continued this pattern in subsequent years. Those still classified as underclassmen had failed most of their ninth year classes.

The planning committee tried to devise a grant proposal to fund strategies to increase the number of incoming students passing all subjects and reduce the number failing most of their classes (see chapter 12 for the special award aspects of the grant). The grant program ended several years later, but Mr. Thelen's goal to target ninth year students lasted throughout his tenure as principal. He and his staff devised many cost-free strategies to help incoming students acclimate themselves to the new world of high school. Their first strategy was to implement two orientation programs, one in the late spring and the other on the day before students reported to school in the fall.

The spring program had two purposes. First, the school wanted to administer placement tests in language arts, mathematics, and foreign language to better program incoming students and reduce the need for class changes in the fall. This was a real issue, as often middle school transcripts arrived in the school without eighth grade scores. In addition, there was often a disjunction between report card grades and student performance on standardized test scores.

Having its own tests provided the school with another way to determine appropriate placement. The school administered these tests on a Saturday morning in June. Student attendance was voluntary, but letters sent to parents stressed that these tests were the only way the school could insure students had the proper programs in September. Eighty percent of the incoming students attended, most accompanied by one or more parents. While the students sat for the tests, the principal and his staff provided an orientation program for the parents.

The orientation began with an auditorium presentation beginning shortly after the students went up to the classrooms for their placement tests. The principal welcomed these parents to the school and thanked them for taking the time to bring their children. This was followed by sundry remarks, common to the remarks most principals probably make to their incoming parents:

- The transition to high school is the most difficult school transition for your children—and for you—so far.
- Your children enter high school as children 13 or 14 years of age. They leave at 17 and 18 as young adults on the verge of attending college, entering the workforce, or joining the military. These four years fly by. You must help your children as they mature into young adults by giving them more responsibility for themselves while understanding that they continue to need your support, even when they do not want it.
- The best advice I can give you is that no matter how difficult your child can be (and teenagers are difficult—at least, I know mine were), always leave the communication channels open. Every day, try to talk to your child for at least 15 minutes. Talk about anything, but talk. Ask about school and friends and likes and dislikes. If you feel there is a problem, do not hesitate to call the school to make an appointment with your child's guidance counselor.
- Your children will face a program of studies more intense than anything you or I had when we went to high school, so do believe your children when they tell you that school is difficult. At some of our fall Parent Association meetings, we will have presentations on different subject areas to explain the curricula and show you the types of questions your child will be facing on the required state exit examinations.
- Understand that your children will have about two hours of homework each night. This includes written work, reading, and studying. You can help by providing a quiet place to study and limiting household chores, videogame and Facebook time, and television viewing. They begin school early, so make sure you have a reasonable lights out time each night.
- While we always welcome you as the parents of our children, please help us to help you. If you need to see someone at the school, please call and

make an appointment so that you will not have to wait when you arrive. Bring a photo ID to the school. This is required of all visitors for the safety of your children.
- Speaking of safety, your child now will be taking trains and/or buses for a long distance. You need to help them learn how to get to school by taking a few trips with them following different routes. You will need to teach them about public transportation safety. When possible, they should always ride with a friend. They should ride in the subway car with the conductor. They should not open purses or wallets in public. They should not wear expensive jewelry.
- If your child has to leave early on any day for any reason, such as a doctor's appointment, remember that you have to come to the school to pick up your child. This is a district regulation—no student may leave the school before the end of his or her regularly scheduled school day unless accompanied by a parent or guardian. You can prevent this problem by scheduling any appointments early in the morning and having your child come to school late, with a doctor's letter of explanation.
- Attend as many Parent Association meetings as possible and definitely come to school on the scheduled parent-teacher conference days. When you come to the school, you send your children the message that school is important. You have been given a copy of the schedule for these meetings; later this morning, the Parent Association officers will tell you more about them.

    This session ended with the different subject area assistant principals, the ninth grade guidance counselor, and Parent Association officers being introduced. Parents were provided with a schedule—they would be attending four 20-minute sessions concerning academics, occupational concentrations, the Parent Association, and guidance/school activities. Each session would give them insights into the targeted area. At the end, they and their children would meet in the cafeteria for light refreshments.
    Yes, this cost money. The principal had to set aside funds to pay staff members to come to school on a Saturday and to pay for the refreshments. However, these costs were insignificant when compared to the benefits for his incoming students and parents.

    In September, staff usually reported to school two days before the first day of classes. This was a transition time for returning staff, for welcomes, professional development workshops, and classroom arrangement. On the second day, the teachers of incoming ninth year students were part of a special orientation program. These new students reported one day before the school officially opened. They received their programs and then reported to the auditorium to meet their principal.

Mr. Thelen introduced the students to the assistant principals. He repeated the items discussed with the parents in language understandable to adolescents. He was positive and supportive, but also realistic and firm. He made the students aware of the importance of doing well in their ninth year and explained how the patterns they established in their ninth year would extend throughout their high school career. He explained the roles of the deans, guidance counselors, assistant principals, and himself. His underlying theme was that the students must begin to take responsibility for their own futures.

After this presentation, the students followed their programs for shortened 15-minute periods. They learned how to navigate around the school (Mr. Thelen and his assistant principals stayed in the hallways to help them on their way) and met their teachers. They ended in the cafeteria where they met their guidance counselor and had lunch before heading home.

Every school and school system has different priorities, rules, and regulations, but every principal needs to greet his incoming students. The days when principals were shadowy figures who lived in a sacrosanct office are long gone. Today's school leader must always be in the forefront, being a role model and setting the tone for the school.

These orientations were followed up by additional "welcoming" strategies during the first weeks of school:

- The principal visited all ninth year English classes, where he reiterated the themes of his opening day remarks and taught a lesson on the importance of the ninth year. This included an explanation of how a GPA is computed, why this average would determine the students' futures, and how poor grades in the ninth year could negatively impact their GPA. Students were given two copies of a summary of this presentation at the end of the period. One they signed, promising that they would take the other home to show to their parents. The signed copy was collected and kept on file in the principal's office.
- The ninth year counselors also visited all classes to review the many transitions the students were facing and explain their supportive roles.

- The deans, accompanied by one or two "super" seniors also visited classes. Here, fifth and sixth year seniors described how they "messed up" their ninth year and how this resulted in their present situation. Their message: Don't make the mistakes we did. The deans followed up by introducing themselves and making students aware that at this school, rules were strictly enforced. They also stressed that students should see them immediately if they were having any problems with other students.
- Ninth year English classes used the school's *Student Handbook* as a text for the first three weeks. Students learned the history of the school and its special programs. Discussions and essays on ethical issues derived from reading the school's rules, regulations, and policies. Teachers led their students on a top to bottom tour of the school. Students were taught how to read a subway map and find alternate travel routes to the school.
- Mr. Thelen's last strategy was not so welcoming, but was effective: The deans targeted incoming students who broke any school rule. The first time students cut a class, they found themselves in the dean's office; often, the cut turned out to have an explanation (for example, the student went to a counselor, but did not follow procedures). However, a message was sent to all students: You don't cut in this school. Likewise, students forgetting ID cards or showing a tendency to come late also found themselves in the dean's office. As much as Mr. Thelen and his staff tried to keep the orientation period positive, they knew that for some students the threat of the dean's intervention was important.

Mr. Thelen also had a major programming goal: To assign the best teachers to the incoming ninth year classes. "Best" was defined as those teachers who had demonstrated the most success with motivating and teaching incoming students. He and his assistant principals had an unwritten rule: If a master teacher wanted a special class (elective, honors, senior, or whatever in the teacher's mind was "special"), they could also expect to have a ninth year class. Over the years, these teachers often involved their freshmen in special programs and projects that made instruction even more exciting.

At this time, most schools in the district reorganized for the spring semester, with students receiving new programs. This was a cost-saving measure: Enrollments in schools decreased from September to January so fewer classes and teachers were needed. Teachers were able to apply for semester sabbaticals only in the spring, offsetting staff loss. To further assist his incoming students, Mr. Thelen set aside funding so that ninth year students remained with the same teachers from September through June. This gave the students more time to adjust, get to know their teachers, and make up for any early deficiencies caused by the trauma of transition to high school.

Later in his tenure as principal, when the district was more flush with money and budgets improved, Mr. Thelen added a half-semester study skills class to the programs of incoming ninth year students. Programmatically, this was accomplished by meshing its time slot with the student's physical education classes. By state regulations, students only needed physical education for half the semester; so, for the other half, the students were given this new course.

In the fall, the curriculum centered on topics such as how to read textbooks, how to take notes, and how to do homework. In the spring, the class was taught in the computer rooms. Students learned the basics of word processing and began doing their assignments using word processing programs. At least one computer room was left open and teacher-supervised for an hour or more after regular classes so students without computer access at home would have a place to use the skills they had learned.

After a year or two, Mr. Thelen found that not all incoming students needed these basic courses. He asked his guidance staff to identify the 30 or so incoming students with the best middle school academic records and then assigned them to special honors study skills classes that centered on higher level skills, such as library and Internet research. This group of special needs students engaged in project-based instruction and often entered state and national scholastic contests.

All these strategies yielded measurable results. The percentage of incoming students passing all classes rose by about 10 percent; the percentage failing three or more classes was significantly reduced; but, the percentage failing one or two classes rose somewhat. He and his staff saw this as a success, as this last group still tended to graduate, if a summer or semester late.

These three components are part of the seven building blocks of school ambience. Four additional components are described in the next chapter.

Chapter Nine

Creating a Positive School Ambience: Support Services, Parental Involvement, Staff Development, and Punitive Measures

After school leaders instill the basic attitudes for school ambience by creating an atmosphere of respect, incorporating ethical thinking into instruction and making sure all students feel welcome, they need to address the roles and needs of different members of the school community. The next four components deal with how support services enhance school ambience; the importance of parental involvement; the need for staff development; and, finally, the role of a school's deans and security staff.

4. *Student Support Services*

The main task of a teacher is to teach. The school leader enables this by budgeting for the support personnel who provide other necessary services for students. Ms. Niles-Perry's first strategy for improving support services was the reorganization and revitalization of her guidance department.

Over a six-year period at her 7–12 Los Angeles school, counseling transitioned into omnibus rather than grade level counseling. Each counselor followed a class from arrival to commencement, taking full responsibility for the students from acceptance to graduation. This added accountability improved the accuracy of student programs and allowed counselors to get to know each student over the course of the six years.

In addition to working with their own caseloads, each counselor conducted small groups for students with similar issues. A counselor trained in grief counseling led sessions for students who experienced the loss of loved ones. Another worked with students exhibiting signs of eating disorders. Another worked with students traumatized by abuse from a family member or boy- or girlfriend.

She also had her counselors move outside their offices to provide whole-class counseling sessions. Counselors efficiently conveyed grade-specific information and reminded students they would see each of them during the semester. Teachers gained a better understanding of the role of the counselors.

After she had been principal for several years, an improved budget enabled Ms. Niles-Perry to add a full-time college/career counselor who had no caseload, but was responsible for preparing students for life after high school. Until then the regular counselor, without expertise in this area, had handled college counseling, to the detriment of students.

Over time the assigned College Counselor became very adept at her job. What began as a way to help seniors through the college application and financial aid processes evolved into a fully developed ninth year through twelfth year program, providing students with an early awareness of college and career requirements. This counselor encouraged students to stretch their aspirations and apply to colleges outside their own city and state and to consider more prestigious universities. She helped them navigate the complex world of scholarships. The scope of college acceptances greatly expanded. There were dramatic increases in the amounts of money students received in scholarship and financial aid.

While the main task of a teacher is to teach, some basic guidance support was provided in the classroom. Students in Ms. Niles-Perry's school had a "family period" two or three times a week throughout their six years. As much as possible, the same "family" teacher remained with cadres of students as they advanced from seventh grade through the twelfth. These teachers came to know their students better than recitation teachers. They could see changes in attitude, demeanor, and achievement. The nature of the family class permitted these teachers to talk one-on-one with students on a regular basis. They could detect incipient problems and make guidance referrals before they reached crisis stage. As the counselor also moved with the students, these "family" teachers were able to develop a strong working relationship with him or her.

In his academic-vocational school, Mr. Thelen did not have a family class, but students often had double-period occupational classes where they worked on individual projects. Within each concentration, students often had the same teacher in sequential years. This very different type of school organization fostered the same type of family atmosphere.

In her middle school, Ms. Hildebrand found that English teachers often gain unique insights into their students through the creative writing assignments submitted. Often, the early signs of future troubles find their way into student essays and journal entries. When problems were detected, students were referred for guidance support.

Students need support in other areas. Ms. Niles-Perry arranged after-school tutorial sessions for students with academic deficiencies. The number and scope of these sessions expanded or contracted depending on her school's allotted budget. After a change in teachers' contracts expanded their day and made tutorial services a part of the regular program, Mr. Chen, principal of a Brooklyn high school, developed procedures for providing help for those students most in need. He supplemented this with targeted tutoring in the weeks before scheduled exit examinations. He created mini-courses to provide opportunities for students to make up for past failures. Good school leaders use whatever means are available to give students every opportunity to pass courses and mandated examinations.

Long before such programs became the vogue, Ms. Rivera's suburban high school had an Executive Partnership Program which paired at-risk students with business executives. An executive followed a student's progress, invited the student to the workplace, and, in a very real sense, became the student's mentor throughout his or her high school career—often through college and even into his or her profession. Begun and run by a very passionate teacher, a career-changer from the business world, the program eventually provided college scholarships to qualified graduates through a special fund set up by the business mentors.

Regardless of the formal support programs provided, students find their own advisors, from the deans (who often make frequent referrals their monitors) to assistant principals, to individual teachers, to school security agents. Every adult in the school must see himself or herself as a part of the support services for children. A student may feel more comfortable sharing a problem with a cafeteria worker than a counselor. This is the final key to improving school ambience through support services: Every child should be able to find at least one caring adult in the school to go to when he or she needs advice.

5. *Parental Involvement*

Ms. Valletta had mixed feelings about parent involvement. She felt that educational decisions should be made by professionals. Parents could provide insights into the needs of their children and should be fully informed of all aspects of the school's educational program, but should parents have a role in hiring staff? Determining a school's budget? Setting educational goals? Determining a school's mission?

She was also concerned about the misuse of parental power by individual parents and advocacy groups. One of Ms. Valletta's superintendents rhetorically asked why every Parent Association president was the parent of a problem child. The superintendent asked this question rhetorically because he knew the answer: The parent sought the position to have special access to the principal and superintendent to advocate for his or her child not only as a parent, but as a Parent Association officer. Some felt that their children should be given special treatment because of their position.

Many urban areas have strong parent advocacy groups whose mission is to serve as watchdogs to be sure no school is harassing students. Unfortunately, many of the students they advocate for are those with decidedly antisocial tendencies, whose very presence in school poses a threat to their peers and a disruption of education. There are no advocacy groups for the vast majority of children and parents who want a safe and supportive environment for learning.

Over time, Ms. Valletta's position on this mellowed as she saw the advantage of a parental presence on the School Leadership Team, the Safety Committee, the Academic Affairs Committee, and hiring committees. The parental presence allowed her to provide parents with a basic education as to how the school operated so they could better understand programs, policies, and decisions. Their presence allowed this principal to fulfill her function as a master teacher in very real ways. Here are some examples.

The School Leadership Team (SLT) is charged with creation of the school budget. In some schools this leads to major donnybrooks, with the team looking to reorganize everything without realizing the consequences of the changes. When Ms. Valletta's team had their first meeting on budget, she began by saying that every number on the budget in front of them stood for a person doing a job for the children of the school, a person who needed this job to support his or her own family. She then explained what each person did.

This was time consuming, but it insured the SLT would not make frivolous or whimsical changes for change's sake. All members realized that any decision would impact the real lives of people. These parents, teachers, students, and administrators came to share in their principal's organic view of the school, better understanding how the school community worked together to provide an education for their children.

The process of hiring new assistant principals in Ms. Valletta's district involves having parents as voting members of the selection committee, along with teachers, other administrators, and, on the high school level, students. Ms. Valletta saw this as another teaching opportunity: What attributes does this school community desire in an assistant principal? What do they see as *necessary* attributes? As *preferred* attributes? What questions should be asked? What types of responses are looked for? By taking the trouble to have a real orientation session, the committee came to a consensus on how to select the best person for vacancies.

This principal learned a good deal from parents during the application reviews and interviews. Parents invariably saw through educational jargon and gobbledygook on resumes and in verbal responses, asking what, exactly, were these candidates saying? Often, even Ms. Valletta could not give an answer. They were astute in seeing how resume organization and presentation and the very dress and demeanor of an applicant often told them more about the candidate than the words written or said.

The parents had an uncanny ability to judge the sincerity of a candidate by applying simple criteria: *If I came to this person with a problem, would he or she solve it for me and my child? Is this a person I can trust?* The students on these committees were equally astute. When rating candidates, parents and students tended to be more critical than the teachers or administrators, usually assigning lower scores to the resumes and interviews.

A principal gains power by sharing knowledge. Taking the time to provide truthful and understandable explanations fosters trust and a belief in the school leader's competence as an educator. Once school leaders gain this trust, they are invested with the power to do what is necessary to move their schools forward and improve teaching and learning.

There is an inverse ratio of parent involvement to the age of their children: the younger the child, the greater the involvement. By the high school years, parent involvement tends to be low. Beginning principals are dismayed by this. In time, they come to see this phenomenon as a natural progression. It is a parent's difficult task to raise and prepare a child to leave the nest to go out on his or her own. In the early years of schooling, parents need to be more nurturing and more involved. As the child gets older, parents need to gradually relax the reins and allow their children to take more responsibility for their education. The students also realize this. Most high schoolers would prefer to handle problems themselves than have their parents intervene.

This dual, but schizophrenic, parental task—to nurture and to let go—should be a major theme of a principal's remarks to parents at a new student/parent orientation. More should be added at the first Parent Association meeting, focusing on the needs of the parents of incoming students. At Mr. Thelen's school, the ninth year guidance counselor made a presentation on what parents could expect from their children as they transitioned into high school: Normal teenage rebellion at the parents' and the school's authority. The counselors described behaviors typical of this rebellion, talked about the peer pressures the students faced, and then alerted parents to behaviors that should trigger a call to them.

How does a principal determine the topics for Parent Association (PA) meetings? Mr. Thelen met with his PA officers in June to determine the topics and dates for the next school year. He knew the school year is cyclic with a constant flux of students and parents (a real turnover every four years in high school) and staff (roughly 5 percent to 8 percent per year). After several years as principal, he saw that topics and issues that were old hat to him were new to the changing population of parents, students, and teachers. Critical topics need to be periodically repeated.

His first PA meeting was always devoted to the needs of the parents of incoming students. Another fall meeting targeted the needs of the parents of juniors and seniors to help them learn about the college application process. A spring meeting was devoted to student performances and included an evening presentation of several student acts from the annual school musical. Other meetings were devoted to topics of interest to parents (what is my child learning in mathematics . . . science . . . social studies . . .). Some were controversial topics, such as sex education and the district's condom availability program. Most meetings were repeated on a two- or three-year cycle.

Sometimes, at the request of the PA officers, he arranged for parenting workshops on helping teenagers deal with peer pressure, identifying eating disorders, etc. Parents trusted Mr. Thelen because he incorporated their suggestions, making it easy for him to set up the meeting schedule and topics for the upcoming school year.

Parent attendance at meetings was never high. In his school of 1,600 students, attendance by 20 parents was a good night (except for those featuring a student performance, when attendance was inflated by the parents of the students in the show). He tried everything to increase this attendance, from flyers sent home with students to having a parent reminder network where parent volunteers (usually the PA officers) called or e-mailed parents to remind them to attend. He experimented with having meetings at different times. Saturday morning meetings were no better attended and drew the same parents who had attended the evening meetings. Meeting attendance was low even when tragedy struck.

In Mr. Thelen's third year, a student from the school was attacked on the subway on her way home from school. She was wearing gold jewelry and was approached by a group of teenagers from another school. When she refused to give up her necklace, a scuffle ensued, an attacker took out a knife and the child was killed. The school immediately initiated grief counseling. Mr. Thelen and his staff developed an instructional piece on safety which resulted in "Safety First" posters going up around the school.

The police department made a special presentation for parents on school safety and keeping children safe, sending several high-ranking officers to a special, well-publicized PA meeting. Despite the seriousness of the issue, only 30 or so parents attended. One parent, who did not attend, later told Mr. Thelen that she felt the incident was unrelated to the school and a tragedy of life in the big city, like so many one reads about in the papers every day.

The "Safety First" poster that resulted from this tragedy can be adapted to schools in different districts and levels.

At special events, such as the school's annual fashion show, Principal Thelen often spoke with parents and asked why he had not seen them at PA meetings. A common response was that since they received periodic newsletters, they did not need to attend. A newsletter was mailed out four times a year. Given the cyclic nature of the school year, there were standard items that appeared in each issue, so that at the appropriate time in the school year parents were made aware of relevant information.

The first newsletter mailed in late August provided the school calendar for the fall semester and the schedule and topics of PA meetings. An article advised parents to have their children always carry an emergency pack that included a transportation card, in case the child lost his or her train/bus pass; five dollars; the work phone number of parents or guardians; and for girls, one or two sanitary pads. Another article provided information on the services of the school clinic and the district's immunization requirements.

Later newsletters provided information on working papers, school activities, testing schedules, district and school regulations, special events, and any items requested by the PA. The last *Parent Newsletter* was a "Highlights of the School Year" issue, a celebration of the successes of students and staff, naming as many individuals as possible.

SAFETY FIRST

The city can be a dangerous place. The police try to make it safer as you travel to and from school. School staff tries to keep the school safe for you. But, YOU are the most important person when it comes to keeping yourself safe. Here's what YOU can do:

ON THE WAY TO SCHOOL
   TRAVEL WITH A FRIEND. If you don't know anyone, see your guidance counselor who will try to pair you with someone who lives near you.
   STAY ON A CROWDED SECTION OF THE SUBWAY PLATFORM. Never wait in a deserted, poorly lit section.
   STAND BACK FROM THE EDGE OF THE PLATFORM.
   TRY TO TRAVEL IN THE CENTER OF A CROWDED TRAIN CAR. If possible, ride in the same car with the conductor.
   LEAVE THE STATION WITH THE CROWD BY THE NEAREST EXIT. Don't linger behind so you have to go up the stairs by yourself.
   DON'T LOITER OUTSIDE THE SCHOOL—ENTER IMMEDIATELY. Go to the cafeteria where you can have an inexpensive breakfast or just relax.

WHILE IN SCHOOL
   FOLLOW YOUR PROGRAM, GO TO ALL YOUR CLASSES. Students who do this rarely have any problems.
   ALWAYS BE SURE YOU ARE IN A SUPERVISED AREA—a classroom, an office, the cafeteria, the library, the study hall.
   NEVER HANG OUT ON THE STAIRWAYS OR IN A DESERTED HALLWAY. Always be sure a member of the school staff is nearby.
   FOLLOW THE INSTRUCTIONS OF SCHOOL PERSONNEL—Assistant Principals, Teachers, Teacher Assistants, School Aides, Maintenance and Cafeteria Personnel.
   ALWAYS CARRY YOUR ID CARD AND PROGRAM CARD.
   REPORT ANY POTENTIAL PROBLEM to the Office of Pupil Personnel, Room XXX; the Dean's Office, Room XXX; the Principal's Office, Room XXX; or any staff member or school security agent.
   IF YOU SEE TROUBLE, WALK THE OTHER WAY.

AFTER SCHOOL IS DISMISSED
   LEAVE IMMEDIATELY. The Officers of the XXth Precinct and the Transit Police know our dismissal times and station uniformed and undercover police in the vicinity of the school and nearby train stations. They will watch out for you if you leave on time.

> LEAVE THE SCHOOL WITH A FRIEND, especially if you stay after school for any activity.
> NEVER HANG OUT IN A DESERTED AREA OF THE SCHOOL. Always stay where there is a staff member present.

Mr. Thelen came to understand that since this newsletter reached virtually all the parents, those having no issues with their children or the school did not feel it necessary to attend the monthly meetings. It was apparent that in one-parent families or families where both spouses worked (about 90 percent of the students' families), giving up evening or weekend time was a major sacrifice. Many families also had a child in middle or elementary school. It was understandable they would choose to attend meetings in the school of the younger child.

Once Mr. Thelen realized he could not significantly increase parental attendance at monthly meetings, he took another tack. He wanted to insure that whenever parents contacted or visited the school for any reason, they would be welcomed with respect and would feel that any problem was resolved to their satisfaction. He served as a role model for his staff, leaving his door open for parents. Nothing was more important than taking a parent's call or seeing a parent who came to the school.

Classes could not be interrupted so a teacher could speak to a parent who came without an appointment. However, other school personnel were available. For example, when a teacher was in the classroom, the appropriate assistant principal spoke with a parent who had a complaint or problem. The assistant principal listened to the parent and promised to investigate and then call the parent later that day or early the next with the resolution. If necessary, he would set up a meeting with the teacher as soon as possible. This procedure worked because these middle managers were adept at conflict resolution.

Mr. Thelen also began a "Contact a Parent a Day" campaign with the entire teaching staff. He had read a study which indicated that the majority of school-to-parent contacts were negative: Johnny was late, Mary was cutting, Jose was failing, etc. As a result, parents often cringed when they received a call, e-mail, or letter from the school. He discussed this with the staff at an opening conference in September and asked that each staff member contact one parent each day—and not necessarily with bad news. The teacher could call to say that Johnny had been on time for two weeks, that Mary had attended every class last month, or that Jose had passed his last test.

If all staff members did this, 500 parents would be contacted every week, 2,000 every month, 20,000 every school year. Of course, not everyone would make a contact every day, but even 50 percent compliance would lead to significant parental contacts in addition to the usual contacts teachers and counselors made when there were problems.

In any given week, few parents called Mr. Thelen or came to see him. His teachers, counselors, and assistant principals were adept at resolving the issues parents brought to them. The fewer the contacts he had from parents, the better school personnel were responding to parental concerns.

Whenever possible, he and his staff tried to celebrate the successes of students. The printed programs for events with student participants listed the names of all students involved, making these booklets of pride for the parents of these students—items they could show their friends and neighbors. Awards Night gave parents a chance to see their children honored and receive the usual bumper sticker about their child being an honor student. Parents were invited to art gallery openings, portfolio presentations, and annual performances to celebrate the success of their children.

School leaders want to share their expertise. They want parents who join the PA or various school committees to find that knowledge of the operations of the school is open to them and that their ideas on budget, hiring, and school policies are valued. They want parents who attend meetings to learn about age-appropriate student issues, the school's educational program, and topics of importance at specific stages of their children's school career.

Such school leaders keep parents informed through newsletters, and they continually update information on their school's website. They insure that parents who contact the school are listened to with respect and have their problems resolved. The successes of their children are publicly celebrated and acknowledged. School leaders who do all this will find that parents' trust in the staff and leadership of the school is enhanced, improving the ambience of the school.

6. *Staff Development*

There are many books that deal with staff development, and most school districts have their own professional development leaders and programs. A staff development program for new teachers has already been described in chapters 5, 6, and 7. Interpersonal facets of professional development are addressed in *Creating a Successful Leadership Style: Principles of Personal Strategic Planning* (Rowman & Littlefield, 2011), the companion to this book. The following short section will touch on some underlying principles for professional development.

Competent school leaders design professional development to help all members of the school community understand their contribution to the education and well-being of children. The school staff needs to realize that students and parents are their clients and that it is their job to serve these clients to the best of their ability. They do this by being caring, understanding and respectful, by providing the best instruction possible, and by going the extra mile to help a child. Each staff member will fulfill these goals to different degrees.

The school is a reflection of society, although one would hope it is a reflection of society's higher ideals rather than its everyday reality. There are no statistics that can measure how well school leadership instills professionalism and idealism in a staff. It is more a feeling school leaders get as they walk through the halls of a school, looking at interactions between members of the school community, seeing the response of students to instruction, noting whether most people have smiles or frowns.

Looking back on her career as a principal, Ms. Valletta felt that her role modeling, her individual conversations with staff, and her workshops were the major means by which she changed the attitudes of the staff members she inherited. She had found that the majority of these hard-working professionals were doing excellent jobs. Others improved under her administration; others were still borderline, but did not warrant an Unsatisfactory rating and removal. As she neared retirement and looked back at the mosaic of her school, she knew it was working, despite a few rough spots.

Her most important work was with her new hires. They became true professionals under her tutelage. They shared her vision, understood her decisions, and came to her with their problems. At the time of her retirement, she had hired and trained over 60 percent of the staff. Many were or would shortly become assistant principals in the school, training a new generation much as she had trained them. Good schools create a continuing a cycle of hiring and training teachers to maintain their vision and ambience.

7. *Punitive Measures*

Schools are flawed. Budgets always fall short of need. School leaders, teachers, parents, and students are human. In addition to all the positive measures taken to insure a good school ambience, the school leader must also have punitive strategies to deal with the most antisocial and recalcitrant staff and students.

School systems routinely remove or change superintendents when superintendents fail to meet system-wide goals or run afoul of the political machinations of the school board. Superintendents remove principals who are unable to move a school forward despite supports provided. Principals train assistant principals and other administrative staff members to become leaders who promote the vision of the school. They seek to find their strengths and use them to help the school achieve this vision. If assistant principals are unable to fulfill their functions, the principal needs to remove them. Continuing down the chain of command, assistant principals work with their principals to remove incompetent teachers.

If there are punitive measures for trained professionals—who, one should expect, should not need such measures—how can there not be punitive measures for students who are still not ethically or socially mature? Who rebel publicly against authority? For most, this is harmless and acceptable high jinks, ones that adults address with an inner and knowing smile. For a few students, this takes the form of dangerous and disruptive behaviors requiring strong preventative and punitive measures.

To have a positive ambience, the school must be a safe place. System-wide disciplinary regulations must be enforced. School rules that emanate from these regulations need to be thoughtfully formulated and implemented. A principal must insure that the school has sufficient personnel charged with the security of the school: security guards, deans, school aides, assistant principals. Each needs to know his or her role for maintaining safety and discipline. Each needs to be part of a team that consistently enforces the rules and regulations.

As explained in the next chapter, all procedures, rules, and regulations need to be codified. They should be included in a teacher handbook that reflects the thinking of representatives of the school community. The principal should include the same information in a student handbook in a form accessible to students and their parents.

The task of the school security team can be simply summarized: To insure that the few students who are dangerous or disruptive are kept under control. In Mr. Thelen's academic-vocational school, the deans were directed to house-suspend these students and call in their parents for every offense so that the parents, tired of losing time from work, would choose to transfer them to another school.

Each case was as different as each child, but the principal found that most fit into certain categories:

- The parent wanted the student to attend this school, but the child wanted to go elsewhere, usually where her friends were. Acting out was the child's way of expressing her displeasure. Mr. Thelen sympathized with these students. Most students applied to his school because they liked one of the required occupational sequences. However, a child not interested in this aspect of the school's program found such courses irrelevant and boring. The counselors would work with the children and parents to help them resolve their issues as to which school the children should attend. The children would be made aware that the school they wished to attend might not accept them with a failing ninth year record, so they had to study and pass their classes if they wanted a transfer.
- The child wanted to be in the school and truly enjoyed the occupational program. However, either he saw no value in the academic classes or felt he could not succeed. Typically such a child did well in his vocational sequence, but cut or was inattentive or disruptive in academic classes. Mr. Thelen also sympathized with this child. The school accepted students on the basis of their vocational interest and talents, not their academic ability. Many were adept vocationally, but poor academically. Their learning modalities were not verbal or mathematical.

  The guidance counselor and often vocational teachers intervened, helping the students realize that any occupational goals they had would be dashed without a high school diploma. The presenters from different vocational fields emphasized the same when they visited classes. Academic teachers tried to use other learning modalities in their instruction, knowing, however, that the required standardized exit exams were all verbal or mathematical. In many cases, the child struggled but met the academic requirements after continued intervention. Unfortunately, some did not and eventually dropped out or transferred.
- There were family and social issues interfering with the child's education. The school could help with some such problems but, with limited resources, most of these children were referred to outside agencies for counseling, with varying degrees of success.

  Sometimes these social issues involved problems with other students which resulted from neighborhood disputes, or were of the school-related "he said, she said" variety. The school used peer mediation, guidance, and dean interventions. However, sometimes the enmity between students was so great, a transfer of one of the parties was the only solution. On rare occasions, the school had a student who had gotten involved with a gang;

fortunately, local police Youth Officers were usually able to intervene with gang members to safely extricate the child.
- Finally, as in every school, there were students who were predators and whose main reason for coming to school was to bully, to rob, to disrupt. Often some of the previous mentioned reasons were part of their issue, but they carried their response beyond any acceptable range. If allowed to continue unchecked, they would encourage borderline students to take the same negative path and jeopardize the safety of the school. The deans and security agents knew who these students were and apprehended them for every offense, from simple cutting to cursing a teacher to bullying students. The students and their parents got tired of suspensions and hearings and sought greener pastures in which to wreak their mayhem.

For many years, there was a group of such disruptive students in Mr. Thelen's district who were moved by the district from school to school on the premise that a change of venue and removal from their like-minded associates would help them do better. This was rarely the case, but Mr. Thelen felt his school did better than most in working with those students who were the followers of the troublemakers. Since his school did not tolerate the initiators of trouble, students who were easily led into mischief in their previous school found more positive paths to follow. Sometimes, however, Mr. Thelen was given a student with whom he could do nothing and was not even told why the student had been removed from the previous school, such as when he was sent a convicted juvenile arsonist. Fortunately, the juvenile arsonist was apprehended after only a few small trashcan fires.

If schools were given significantly greater resources to target this small but very troubled population, other strategies could be employed. Most schools have barely enough funding to provide basic services for students. For better or worse, these limited funds must be targeted where they can do the most good.

Together, these seven components are crucial to the ambience of a school. They need to move from the mind of the school leader to the formal and informal plans described in the next chapter.

Chapter Ten

Establishing Formal and Informal Systems for Creating a Positive School Ambience

A school must be structured with formal and informal lines of support and authority to maintain its ambience on a day-to-day basis. The following plans implement the seven components described in the last two chapters.

THE SCHOOL'S FORMAL PLAN FOR CREATING A POSITIVE SCHOOL AMBIENCE

Written documents are required to codify a school's expectations, rules, and regulations. If these formal documents are well thought out and include the input of the appropriate members of the school community, they create the framework for positive school ambience. Most of these documents have been mentioned in previous chapters. The first part of this chapter is intended to summarize how these documents work together to create the formal plan.

1. *The Teacher Handbook*

Some schools issue memos at various times during the school year to make sure staff are kept informed. In part, this is a legal issue. In most districts, principals are required to inform staff of key regulations and policies each year.

Issuing memos is not particularly effective. Teachers go to their mailboxes, find them stuffed with papers, sift quickly through the items, and dispose of most of them. If a legal issue arises and the teacher's defense is "I was never informed," a principal cannot prove that the item in question was placed in the mailbox. Duplicating the same memos year after year wastes reams of paper—definitely not "green." Today, many school leaders e-mail memos. They forget that teachers may treat them as spam. While a principal could prove an item was sent, he cannot prove it was opened or read.

One of Ms. Rivera's first projects as principal was the creation of a teacher handbook. She asked members of her cabinet (assistant principals, the union representative, and the coordinator of student activities) and the Academic Affairs Committee (with representatives from staff, students, and parents) for ideas for this handbook. She also looked at the many memos issued each year. She made a list of items to include in the handbook. She sorted these items into categories and wrote rough drafts of the various sections. She sent these "chapters" to the persons most concerned with each (e.g., a copy of the section on support services went to the assistant principal of guidance, the guidance counselors, and the assistant principal of special education).

Ms. Rivera read the corrections and suggestions and put everything together into a single cohesive document, which was then sent to all the assistant principals and the union representative for another reading. After revisions were made, the *Teacher Handbook* was duplicated and ready to give to staff when they reported back in September.

The content and use of the handbook was the topic of the first day's staff meeting. Each staff member received a book and signed a receipt kept on file by the principal. This receipt stated that the staff member received the handbook, would make him- or herself aware of its contents and would read any updates that appeared in the Weekly Bulletin. This bulletin was the one memo the principal still issued each week. It outlined events for the current week, referred staff to sections of the *Teacher Handbook* and provided updates. The textbox below provides an example.

WEEKLY BULLETIN: WEEK BEGINNING DECEMBER XX

MONDAY, DECEMBER XX: Regular Bell Schedule
TUESDAY, DECEMBER XX: Regular Bell Schedule
WEDNESDAY, DECEMBER XX: Regular Bell Schedule; Uniform Examinations
THURSDAY, DECEMBER XX: Regular Bell Schedule; Uniform Examinations
FRIDAY, DECEMBER XX: Regular Bell Schedule; Uniform Examinations

WEEKLY BULLETIN NOTES

1. *Batten Down the Hatches!*
   - The Winter Recess begins 3:15 on Friday. Please be sure that all school equipment and important records are LOCKED in a secure cabinet or locker. THE SCHOOL IS NOT RESPONSIBLE FOR ANY PERSONAL BELONGINGS LEFT IN THE SCHOOL.
   - Please help our custodial staff on Friday. If you are the last teacher in a classroom, have the students empty any trash from the desks. Have the students turn their chairs over on top of the desks at the end of the period. Thank you.

2. *Reminder: Chancellor's Regulation C-105*
   Please review all of Section 9, Legal Matters, in your Teacher Handbook. You are responsible for knowing and implementing all these policies and regulations. Please note one of the newer items, C-105. If any district employee is arrested for any reason, the arrest must be reported IMMEDIATELY to the Office of Personnel Investigations, (XXX) XXX-XXXX, and IMMEDIATELY AND IN WRITING to the Principal. This reminder falls under the provision of protect yourself: Even if the arrest is eventually dropped, not reporting it as required by regulation can result in serious consequences.

3. *Please Announce in All Period 3 Classes: Student Lockers Must Be Left Open!*
   All student lockers must be emptied and left open over the Winter Recess so that the custodial staff may properly clean the school. The school takes NO RESPONSIBILITY for the loss of any items left in the lockers. Locks left on the lockers may be clipped to facilitate cleaning.

4. *Holiday Song Fest*
   Following what has become a tradition, on Friday, December XX, beginning at 7:30, staff members will gather in our lobby to welcome students with a medley of festive songs. Mr. XXXXX, who began this tradition several years ago, is organizing this event. Please see him if you would like to join in the fun. A good singing voice is NOT a requirement.

5. *Spring Professional Assignments*
   - Professional assignments are intended for the entire school year. However, it is possible for you to change your assignment for the coming spring semester. If you wish to do so, please send a letter to

(continued)

the principal specifying what assignment you now have and what assignment you would like for the spring semester. Send a copy of this letter to the union representative.
- Please Note: As you are aware, under IDEA, general education teachers need to participate in IEP conferences. In addition, teachers in inclusionary model classes should be consulting with one another and, on occasion, attending special education staff development meetings. No teacher is expected to do this on his/her prep or lunch period. When such meetings are required, the teacher is excused from his/her professional assignment.

6. *Classroom Door Window Panels*
Do not cover up the door windows to your classroom. There are two reasons for this:

- First, for your own safety and protection, there should be visual access to your room from the hallway.
- Second, every morning, seven days a week, the custodial staff visually inspects all classrooms, even those not used for evening programs. It is a great time saver if they can simply look into rooms not used.

If there is no visual access to your room, please correct this situation immediately. Thank you for your cooperation.

7. *Storm Day Procedures*
Please look over Item 1.4.3 (pages 5 and 6) of the Teacher Handbook regarding Storm Day Procedures. Pay careful attention to the policy regarding a delayed school opening announced by the district. A summary of these procedures has been mailed home to parents.

8. *Make-Up Work*
Please review Item 2.3 (pages 11 to 15) of the Teacher Handbook regarding procedures for make-up work. As per the Fall Calendar, the last day make-up work will be accepted is **Thursday, January XX**. Please make students aware of your make-up procedures and this cutoff date NOW.

9. *Holiday Parties*
As the winter recess approaches, some staff members like to reward students with a special party. This is a wonderful idea. HOWEVER, all staff members are reminded of some simple guidelines to follow for such parties:

- They must be AFTER the 9th period. A party during the regular school day makes it difficult for other teachers to conduct their classes.

(continued)

- The party must be visible through the door window.
- There must be adequate adult supervision.

10. *Clear the Halls!*
Many teachers make it part of their routine to clear the halls outside their classrooms at the late bell and usher in any malingering students. This is the most effective way to keep the halls clear. All staff members should make this a part of their daily routine, especially during the holiday season when student spirits are running high.

11. *Uniform Examinations*
A Parent Newsletter was mailed home two weeks ago. It contained the following message from the principal: On Wednesday, 12/XX, Thursday, 12/XX, and Friday, 12/XX, your child will be taking major examinations in all classes. The marks earned will help teachers determine final grades. Over the next few days, I will be getting calls from some parents asking that their children be excused on these days so they can start their winter recess early. My answer will always be "NO." We try to teach students that school is important. What message are some parents sending their children when they ask that they be given days off? Children in the U. S. attend school for fewer days than children in any other industrialized nation in the world, only 180 or so days each year. Each of these days is important, especially when major examinations are being given.

12. *Items for this Weekly Bulletin and the Highlights Brochure*
If there is any event of school-wide interest that you would like noted in this bulletin, please give a written description of it to Ms. XXXXX in Room 819 by Wednesday afternoon. The item should be clear and concise.

    If you know of any Highlight of the school year that should be included in our Highlights public relations brochure, please send the principal a written description; include the correctly spelled names of all students and staff members involved.

Of course after reading the handbook, some staff members felt that more information belonged in the book, and the principal was besieged with additional items for inclusion. Since the book was issued in a three-ring binder to allow for the removal and addition of pages, updates and changers were easy to make. After three years, it became hard to keep track of the many changes. Ms. Rivera published a second, updated edition. The interest of the staff in expanding the scope and content of the handbook was an indication that they valued this compendium of information on the school.

2. *The Student Handbook*

Some schools give each student a student handbook and calendar notebook every year. Students have a reference book for school information and a daily calendar on which to record assignments, scheduled exams, and important events. This is a yearly expense for the school; or, in the case of private schools, for the student. Most public schools do not have the budget for this. Ms. Rivera created a *Student Handbook* following a pattern similar to the one used to create her *Teacher Handbook*. It was issued to all students; then, in future years, only to incoming freshmen.

The booklet included information relevant to students and their parents, such as graduation requirements, the discipline code, dress code, attendance regulations, clinic services, breakfast and lunch programs, co- and extracurricular activities, a simple floor plan of the school, how to get to the school by public transportation, regulations governing the issuance of working papers, and tips on how to study and succeed. Since personnel changes but offices remain the same, the booklet provided office locations. The names of staff members were not used in the text. Each year, a one-page supplement was issued with the names of key school personnel.

As was done in Mr. Thelen's school, Ms. Rivera used this *Student Handbook* instructionally to orient her incoming students. She designed much of it to help them with their transition to middle and high school. The final page was a parent verification form that the child returned to the school. Parents' signatures verified that their children had showed them the handbook.

Legally, students and their parents were made aware of everything they needed to know about the school and district. However, Ms. Rivera and her staff went beyond legalities to make this booklet a positive statement about the school. From its welcoming remarks by the principal, to the history of the school, to helping students find their way, to informing students how they could get help, to providing guidelines for success, to giving rationales for each school rule, the *Student Handbook* was designed to tell students in a subtle manner that this school had an ambience of safety and success.

School leaders need to develop such handbooks, the content of which will vary from school to school and district to district. Once developed, mere distribution is not enough. The school must use the handbook to help students come to better know the school, mainly as part of transitional orientation. The school must also insure that parents know the handbook exists and have access to it.

3. *The School Safety Plan*

Even before 9/11, each New York City school was required to have a formal School Safety Plan. The Department of Education collaborated with the police department to create a template for each school's mandated Safety Committee to complete. In today's world, similar procedures exist in most school districts.

Most of the information was standard, including fire-drill procedures, designated fire exits, school personnel serving as contact persons for various types of emergencies, and school evacuation procedures in the event of a power failure or other unsafe conditions. Later, procedures for dealing with armed intruders and terrorist attacks were added. Much of this information also appeared in various guises in both the teacher and student handbooks. However, the School Safety Plan was the written formalization of what every good teacher knows is his or her main responsibility: the safety of children.

4. *The Parent Handbook and/or Newsletters*

High school principal Thelen never had occasion to create a parent handbook. Parents had access to the information they needed to know through the *Student Handbook*. In addition, he composed and mailed a "Parent Newsletter" several times a year. This newsletter included information parents needed at different points in the school year as well as articles on timely topics. The Parent Association contributed items or requested information on specific topics. For the high school level, he felt this was sufficient.

In an elementary school, a student handbook would be short and simple, given the age and understanding of the students. Elementary school principals should opt for a formal parent handbook. As mentioned, the younger the children, the greater the parent involvement. Such a handbook would channel this involvement and anticipate and address problems in key areas, such as parental responsibility for dropping off and picking up children. A section on parent volunteerism would be appropriate.

The principal of the middle school could opt for either handbook, or both.

THE SCHOOL'S INFORMAL PLAN FOR CREATING A POSITIVE SCHOOL AMBIENCE

The components of the formal school plan provide staff, students, and parents with written documents that specify procedures for most situations.

They also make sure that appropriate parties are aware of their legal obligations. Taken together, the formal documents provide the school community with a blueprint for almost all contingencies.

However, every school, regardless of size, has an informal network that parallels the formal network but may work more efficiently. A school, like any organization, is a bureaucracy. The informal system cuts through the layers of bureaucracy and provides direct access to the person or persons most able to solve problems. Here are some examples of representative informal systems.

Principals cannot personally handle every issue that arises in a school. If they try, other important aspects of their jobs do not get done. They would have no personal lives. Most formal systems in a school create ladders whereby different members of the school community handle issues and problems at a lower level. Only those not solved by others reach the principal at the top rung. A less euphemistic way of putting this would be to say that levels of bureaucracy buffer the principal from the majority of day-to-day problems. At the same time, the principal does not want to be isolated from the school community. A balance must be struck.

As a principal, Mr. Pfizer established such ladders at his Midwestern middle school. For example, if students or parents had a complaint about a teacher, the formal procedure required they speak with the teacher to try to resolve the matter. If this was unsuccessful, they would speak with the assistant principal who supervised the teacher. If this was unsuccessful, they would speak to Mr. Pfizer. In addition to not being able to handle all problems himself, he had two other reasons for this procedure. First, most issues are best resolved at the lowest possible level. Second, if he were the first person a student or parent spoke with and he was unable to resolve the issue, the only appeal left would be to the district office.

No teacher or assistant principal or principal wants a problem settled by a higher authority. It is best to settle the matter before it moves to the next rung on the ladder. Mr. Pfizer held workshops with his new teachers on resolving complaints. His assistant principals only referred matters that they felt required a principal's input. Before the parent or student came to Mr. Pfizer's office, the assistant principal filled him in on all aspects of the problem.

There were exceptions. If a parent or student came directly to him, Mr. Pfizer always welcomed him or her. He would listen, take notes, and promise to resolve the issue in a timely fashion. Where feasible, he would accompany the parent or student to the office of the person he felt would be able to handle the problem.

In a typical week, few parents or students came to his office. He used this time to develop proactive strategies to reach out to students. During the school year, he conducted lessons for each grade level to provide students with grade appropriate information, encourage them to succeed, and increase his own visibility. For example, he spoke to his graduating eighth graders about the high school application process and the types of changes they could expect in their new schools.

Many high school principals take a similar proactive approach. Mr. Thelen had no difficulty determining what he would say to his incoming students (the importance of succeeding in the ninth year and school supports available); his tenth graders (as several required state exams were given that June, he stressed the importance of passing exams and courses to move into the upper grades); and his twelfth year seniors (avoiding "senioritis," graduating on time, the college application process).

However, aside from advising his eleventh year students to enter the senior year with no deficiencies, he had trouble finding a topic for his eleventh year lesson until he came upon an anonymous Internet document that purported to duplicate a speech given at a high school by Bill Gates. Mr. Thelen used this to motivate a lesson on the importance of taking personal responsibility. The textbox below duplicates the handout he gave to these students.

This may be a modern Internet legend, but the story goes that Bill Gates (Harvard's most famous drop-out), in the not-so-distant past, gave a speech at some unspecified high school in which he talked about how our feel-good, politically correct test-oriented schools are creating a generation of children with no concept of the real world. According to the legend, he gave his student audience 10 rules (I've seen versions with more or fewer rules) they probably never learned in school.

Rule 1: Life is not fair. Get used to it!
Rule 2: The world won't care about your self-esteem. The world will expect you to accomplish something before you feel good about yourself.
Rule 3: If you think your teacher is tough, wait 'til you get a boss.
Rule 4: Flipping burgers is not beneath your dignity. Your grandparents had a different word for burger flipping: They called it "opportunity."

(continued)

> Rule 5: If you mess up, it's not your parent's fault, so don't whine about your mistakes.
> Rule 6: Before you were born, your parents weren't as boring as they are now. They got that way from paying your bills, cleaning your clothes and listening to you talk about how cool you think you are. So, before you save the rain forest from the parasites of your parent's generation, try delousing the closet in your own room.
> Rule 7: Your school may have done away with winners and losers, but life has NOT. In some schools, they have abolished failing grades and they'll give you as many times as you want to get the right answer or earn a passing grade. This doesn't bear the slightest resemblance to anything in real life.
> Rule 8: Life is not divided into semesters. You don't get summers off, and very few employers are interested in helping you find yourself. Do that on your own time.
> Rule 9: Television is NOT real life. In real life, people actually have to leave the coffee shop and go to their jobs.
> Rule 10: Be nice to nerds. Chances are you'll end up working for one.

As you might imagine, he and his juniors had quite a lively discussion.

Principals cannot personally handle every issue one-on-one. But, they can make themselves visible to every student and use their teaching ability to encourage them to work hard, study, and graduate. The principals mentioned above believed that these informal visits helped improve the ambience of their schools better than formal written documents.

No matter how good the ambience of any school, there always has to be one person in the school no student wants to see. In Mr. Thelen's school, this was Mr. Flint, his AP/Security. Mr. Flint was tall and imposing. But rather than use the threat of physical punishment, he used ingenious strategies so that students never wanted to find themselves referred to his office.

Mr. Flint was the school's liaison with the local police station. Almost every day, the local Youth Officers visited his office. Often, they collaborated in dealing with a student who may have engaged in some mischief such as graffiti, petty theft, fighting, etc. Such acts were rare but beyond the more minor infractions that the deans routinely handled, so these students were sent to Mr. Flint. He would often read to them from the state's penal code. He had a copy on his desk but sometimes his "readings" were extemporaneous creations designed to put the fear of the law into perpetrators. The Youth Officers would solemnly nod their heads in agreement and describe the dire consequences of such acts. By this time, most students would be quaking in their shoes, wondering if they would be getting five or ten years. Of course, by "special arrangement," Mr. Flint would help them "get off" this time with a little detention, an apology, and some school service.

One story concerning Mr. Flint originated before Mr. Thelen became principal and was already part of the mythology of the school. Mr. Flint asked a teacher who was an amateur electrician to create a "lie detector." This was a wooden box with green and red lights on the top and a buzzer inside. Control buttons were under Mr. Flint's desk and attached by wire. When students accused of more serious incidents were sent to Mr. Flint, he had them hold a wire emanating from the front of the box and told them that if they told him a lie, a buzzer would sound and the red light would blink. Of course, the wire was a fake, not connected to anything. The buzzer and red light were controlled by the buttons under Mr. Flint's desk.

Word permeated the student body that no one could get away with anything because Mr. Flint always knew who was telling lies. After a few weeks, however, the principal ordered Mr. Flint to stop using his machine, as several parents had complained to the district that their children were being given a lie detector test illegally.

Most students referred to Mr. Flint once never did anything to be referred again. He used his reputation to become another factor in the school's plan to help freshman learn its strict rules. The first time a ninth year student cut a class, Mr. Flint personally saw him or her, read the riot act, called the parent, and put the student "on probation." Most never cut again.

Very difficult students were often in Mr. Flint's office, having their parents called time and time again, until the parents got tired of missing work and decided to transfer their children to other schools. Sometimes, however, such students became his monitors. He kept tabs on them to make sure they were going to class, doing their work, and staying on the straight and narrow. He called parents and kept them informed of their children's progress. In later years, many such students returned to the school to thank Mr. Flint for setting them straight. Without him, they never would have graduated.

Mr. Flint sometimes caused Principal Thelen problems by, perhaps, going a bit overboard. He could suffer from "Dean's Syndrome," sometimes assuming the worst of good students. This matter is discussed in *Creating a Successful Leadership Style: Principles of Personal Strategic Planning* (Rowman & Littlefield, 2011).

Some difficult students become monitors for assistant principals, deans, and teachers. Giving such students a sense of worth and responsibility often helps them succeed. They also help the school informally as spies. Such reformed mischief makers have their eyes and ears in all the right places. Because of their information, major problems, such as students preparing for a fight, can be stopped before they happen. Nothing in the written material will mention this as a contributing factor to a positive school ambience. Neither will you read about staff members listening to the conversations of their student monitors.

Finally, school ambience often comes down to the unique talents and skills of individual staff members which, when taken together, have an enormous impact. These talents and skills will vary with the personnel found in each school.

Ms. Valletta's five security guards had uncanny powers of observation. They would always keep track of students as they entered the school, focusing on the known problem students. If there was an incident in the school and the victim described the perpetrator as someone in jeans with a green sweatshirt, the guards knew who to look for. They knew what students carried as they entered and left the school. If a student entered with an empty book bag and a loosely hanging coat but left with a full book bag and a coat that looked like a blown-up balloon, they inferred that the student was leaving with stolen items, and were usually correct in this assumption.

One of Ms. Valletta's guards, David, had been a graffiti "artist" in his misspent youth. Whenever graffiti appeared on a wall or desk, he knew how to quickly determine the "artist." The combined talents of this group made the school more secure and safer for all.

Students are often helped by the talents of particular staff members who go beyond their job descriptions. One of Ms. Niles-Perry's guidance counselors was an expert in helping students (and staff) deal with the loss of a family member or close friend. When students were grieving, she knew how to help them cope and, if necessary, referred them for more intense assistance to out-of-school agencies. Another counselor was an expert in helping students deal with eating disorders, a growing issue in the school and society.

A third was expert in dealing with the victims of bullying. Whether a student was or was not in the designated caseload was irrelevant.

While all of Mr. Chen's deans did their jobs well, some were more astute at dealing with particularly sensitive matters and difficult parents. He knew he could turn to Fran or Ora for the most difficult issues. They were adept in procedures involving superintendent's suspensions. They fully prepared the school's case and made succinct and organized presentations at the district office. The hearing officer agreed with the school in almost every case. Jean, one of the cafeteria deans, saw all students as her children, and in addition to making lunch a pleasant time for all students, provided advice and help to students.

A teacher in Ms. Rivera's school began the Executive Partnership Program, pairing at-risk students with business executives, long before such programs became commonplace. Another ran a successful Drama Club and another began a Photography Club, both of which encouraged students to attend school on a regular basis and do better in their studies. Their work is representative of the fine work done by all advisors of after-school activities and all coaches of varsity and intramural teams.

Mr. Thelen's occupational teachers often had students for double periods over multiple semesters. They came to know their students and their parents very well and could prevent small problems from becoming big ones through their own intervention or by referral to the guidance counselors.

In every school, different assistant principals use their strengths to do different tasks from patrolling the hallways to training teachers to supervising the school store to organizing special student events to finding more business partners. Every school with a positive ambience has a critical mass of teachers, counselors, assistant principals, aides, security agents, custodial helpers, and cafeteria workers who care and give of themselves.

Two other important components of school ambience are the school's physical plant and its custodial staff. They are the subject of the next chapter.

The creation of a positive school ambience is an art. It does not happen overnight, but evolves over time. It depends on having a professional staff who truly care about students and school leaders who are role models for both staff and students. It begins with good instruction that includes basic ethical principles. It has formal documents to define roles and clarify procedures and an informal system that utilizes the unique talents of individual staff members.

Chapter Eleven

Working with the Custodian and Physical Plant

The preparation of candidates for school leadership positions includes the topics in this text plus many others, everything from interpersonal relations, to staff and curriculum development, to management tools and techniques, to collaborative leadership, to developing and implementing a vision. However, few texts deal with the actual physical plant of the school and the sometimes ambiguous relationship between the school community and custodian. Yet these are important factors in the creation of a positive school ambience.

Much of this book is devoted to talking about strategies various school leaders use to help make their schools work well for students and teachers. Underlying the success of some schools are two "givens" over which the school leader has no control: its location (and related feeder school patterns) and its physical plant.

The location of a school, particularly a large middle or high school, is sometimes determined by the land available to the locality rather than by what is best for students. A school leader who moves from one school to another will find a different ambience because of widely differing locations, feeder school patterns, and physical plants. For this chapter, we will look at the particular to make generalizations applicable to the many. Our example will be Principal Thelen's academic-vocational high school.

Anthony Thelen began teaching in a very large school in upper Manhattan. West Side High School was built on a block that, according to the lore of the school when he joined the faculty in 1971, was one of the highest drug-related crime areas in New York City. How to solve this problem? Raze the block and build a school. This did not cause issues, but the feeder school pattern did. As a "neighborhood" school with no special programs, almost all its students came from feeder junior high schools located north of the school in Manhattan or the Bronx. As more and more high schools added special programs or themes, many higher performing students with savvy parents slated for West Side High chose to attend smaller specialized schools. Over time, this left the school with a higher percentage of lower performing and troubled students.

The principal at the time, Mr. White, was a true believer in universal comprehensive education. He felt public schools should welcome all students. He gently railed against the rash of specialty schools and then charter schools that sought to draw better students, leaving the comprehensive high schools with more difficult jobs to do. He believed in the large comprehensive school that offered students many choices and did not adhere to one theme or a few special programs.

As we look back now, he was a voice crying in the wilderness of change, but he and his administration proved that a well-run large school could work for most students. It was only after he and his leadership staff retired that the school began to deteriorate. Today, there is no West Side High. The school plant is now the West Side School Complex housing several smaller schools.

Students brought the issues of the feeder schools and their neighborhoods into Mr. White's school. Twenty or thirty students coming from the same feeder school brought the antipathies and grudges of the eighth grade. Students from the same neighborhoods brought their local squabbles.

If one were to look back at the city in the 1970's, one would see neighborhoods in its poorer sections divided by fluid ethnic and racial boundaries as new waves of immigrants from different countries came seeking better lives. Some of these groups brought ancient conflicts and feuds. At West Side High, every effort was made not to have Dominican students in the same lunch period as Haitian students to reduce the chance of conflict. As the 1970's progressed, such ethnic issues eased, but the interpersonal conflicts from feeder schools and local neighborhoods did not.

Nine years later, when Mr. Thelen began his supervisory career at a mid-sized academic-vocational high school in lower Manhattan, he found a different atmosphere. The school was surrounded by a business district, not a residential neighborhood. Students interested in the theme of the school came from all parts of the city so few were from any one middle school or neighborhood. Interpersonal issues tended to be left outside the school, as its physical plant sent the message that this school was a place for serious business where all who entered came to work.

West Side High School is basically a square box. The walls are painted cinder blocks. It was utilitarian and looked like any other school built in many communities in the 1960's and 1970's. Academic Vocational High, an exquisite example of Art Deco architecture, was build as a WPA project in the Roosevelt years. It is still supported by various segments of the apparel industry (in the 1930's, and still today, New York City was the fashion center of the United States). The outside of the school boasts six large display windows, of the kind found outside department stores such as Bloomingdale's and Macy's. The main entrance with bronze doors is topped by an Art Deco mosaic. Students pass through these doors into an atrium with marble walls and floors and more department store-style display cases.

On their first day in the building, new students continue forward into the auditorium, one of the largest school auditoriums in the city, featuring landmark-status giant murals on either side. The upstairs academic rooms look like classrooms, but with wainscoting and impressive wooden cabinets. The vocational rooms are modeled on the workshops found in the apparel houses of the 1930's. A student first entering this building feels a sense of awe and of history. It is not like any other school these students or most teachers have ever seen.

Mr. Thelen served at Academic Vocational High for 22 years and never ceased to be amazed by the beauty of the place. One of the faculty jokes was that if the city faced a financial crisis, it could sell the school to a developer who would turn it into a luxury condominium. The entrance was impressive; the rooms were large with high ceilings; the building was solid, made with poured concrete; corner rooms had light entering from two sides, perfect for art classes; views of the Empire State Building could be seen from one side of the building and, for a while, views of the Twin Towers from the other. In recent years, former commercial buildings on the same block as the school actually have been converted into high-end condos, so the "joke" has the bite of reality to it.

An impressive building has a positive effect on all who enter and work in it. The custodial staff wants to maintain its beauty. Staff members have a proprietary feeling about their work environment. Students think twice before engaging in vandalism or graffiti since what may be fair game in the typical utilitarian institutional building seems inappropriate in an impressive, well-maintained structure. There were isolated instances of such behavior, but in all cases the culprits were found. The deans and security guards looked upon themselves as preservers of the building and left no stone unturned to protect it.

Drawing from scores of middle schools in all boroughs and having an impressive physical plant greatly reduced vandalism and limited out-of-school strife entering the building. Two other aspects of the school's location and architecture also helped.

The school was in a very low crime area. The local police could devote more person power to the schools within the precinct. Every day, police officers provided safe conduct corridors from school to public transportation at dismissal. Youth Officers and School Liaison Sergeants often visited the school. There was a police presence and frequent patrols when the school had evening events, such as dances and student performances. A call for police assistance led to an almost immediate response. Mr. Thelen always appreciated the presence and help of his local precinct and its dedicated officers.

All school buildings have multiple entrances and exits, all of which must be free to provide emergency egress from the building. You can lock doors to prevent outsiders from entering the building, but they must remain open from the inside to permit exit in case of fire or other peril. Many suburban and rural schools have horizontal plants, spread out over a large area of real estate. Some have 10 or more entrances.

Academic Vocational High is a vertical school with only five entrances: two in the rear of the building, on the east and west wings; two in the front, also on the east and west wings; and the main center entrance in the front. Mr. Thelen and his staff could easily control access and egress. The rear west-wing doors were adjacent to the dean's office. The rear east-wing doors were adjacent to the attendance office and guidance suite. Both doorways had panic bars. If anyone opened them from the inside, a loud alarm would sound, immediately bringing staff from these nearby offices.

School aides sat inside both front-wing entrances. The center entrance was always open. Students, staff, and visitors entered here, past a security desk manned by a guard. All first-floor windows were barred, eliminating them as entry points; nothing could be passed through them as they opened into office spaces used by staff members. One cannot underestimate the importance of having so few entry/exit points so that all can be adequately secured by assigned or proximate staff.

Mr. Pfizer's rural Midwestern middle school had 10 entrances. He did not have the budget to post an aide or security guard at each. Only three had a staffed office nearby. At unguarded exits, students could open the doors and admit other students or intruders undetected. After one serious intruder incident, he locked five of the exits, only to be cited by the local fire department and forced to remove the locks. At the advice of the fire department chief, he put approved panic bars on these entrances. This was safer, as the loud alarm would bring school personnel to the doors. However, Mr. Pfizer knew that in the seconds it took staff to arrive, trespassers could vanish into the nooks and crannies, halls and bathrooms of the building.

There were no further serious incidents and almost all "intruders" were registered students who were late to school or who had cut classes. He began enlisting parent volunteers to guard entrances, but there were days when a parent was absent and the backup could not make it. While his students, staff and parents felt the school was adequately safe and secure, Mr. Pfizer always worried that someday the unimaginable could happen.

Some law enforcement officials and educators think that metal detectors provide the ultimate in school security. It is naive to think schools with metal detectors keep weapons out of the building. Every student knows which exit doors will be unguarded so that a child bent on mischief can admit someone with a weapon at any time. Even if the doors are secure, ground-level windows provide a way for anyone to pass a weapon into the building.

Until there are security cameras at every possible entry point and full-time staff to monitor the screens, there will always be danger. At Academic Vocational High, such danger was minimized because of its physical plant. There was a minor downside. Quickly evacuating a 10-story building in case of emergency takes time. Fortunately, multiple staircases led to the five exit points. Since the school was built almost entirely of concrete, a fire would be slow to spread. With all the security issues raised after Columbine and 9/11, Mr. Thelen was very glad to have five secure exits, an accident of architecture he serendipitously inherited.

Every advantage has its disadvantage. Academic Vocational High is an old school, completed in 1938, with elevators, fixtures, heating, and electrical wiring built to specification for the needs of 1938. Some of the internal architecture, originally designed for a school housing far fewer pupils, is dated and potentially dangerous (such as locker areas in secluded corners of the building).

A school leader can do little with existing internal systems, except try to have them fixed and upgraded as necessary. In the early 1990's, the district generated a plan to use capital funds to upgrade the entire building. An architectural firm was hired and its representatives met with a school committee representing administration, staff, parents, and students. The interior walls were going to be ripped open to upgrade heating and electrical systems anyway, so internal redesign would only be a minor extra. The architects and school community could map out how the inside of the school could be redesigned to meet the needs of students and staff in the next millennium.

The school would be centrally air conditioned. There would be large offices for each department, with computer terminals for the staff and easy access to the book rooms. Occupational rooms would be given new, state-of-the-art equipment (the business advisory board provided suggestions). All classrooms would have computer terminals and the same cutting-edge technology. The cafeteria would have a real kitchen so that food could be prepared onsite instead of being shipped in and reheated on steam tables.

Imagine being given carte blanche to take a 60-year-old building and turn it into a state-of-the-art educational campus. The plans for this renovation, including how it could be done in segments so the school could continue to operate (albeit with a lower enrollment), were drawn up to everyone's satisfaction, at a cost of $600,000. These plans are still gathering dust on top of a file cabinet in back of the principal's office, where Mr. Thelen stored them when the project was scrapped due to lack of capital funds.

Now retired and looking back at this whole fiasco with eyes older and wiser, he's rather glad the school was not changed. There is something majestic, if quirky, about the building. To change it would be like tearing down Yankee Stadium and replacing it with a modern ballpark, minus the ghosts of past teams and players. Unthinkable!

When he moved up from chair to principal, Mr. Thelen toured the school with an assistant principal who had been in the school far longer than he. All school leaders new to a building need to do this to learn about the nooks and crannies of the building as well as its history and lore. For example, Mr. Thelen was told about the helicopter landing pad on the roof of the building, installed so that FDR, running for a third term, could get into and out of the city quickly when he addressed labor union leaders gathered in the auditorium.

In a storage room on the second floor, a floor-to-ceiling mirror covers an entire wall. The story is Balanchine practiced in this room. Finally, the decrepit projection equipment in the rear booth of the auditorium was state of the art in 1940. The auditorium was used on weekends as one of the first film "art houses" in New York City. This was the only tale Mr. Thelen could verify, as long-time neighborhood residents remembered this "theater" from their youth.

Then there were the nooks and crannies. In the basement and sub-basement, this new principal found an unbelievable amount of furniture piled in many spaces —student and teacher desks that had been replaced by newer models, but were still in usable condition—useful knowledge to tuck away for future needs. He also found out that the school was one of the few buildings left in the city heated by steam lines that came in from underground conduits, which explained why the lower floors were tropical while upper floors were ice boxes during the winter months.

He discovered internal air-conditioning vents throughout the school. However, the story goes, as the school was being built in the late 1930's, the district decided it was not politically correct to air-condition a school during the Depression, so no space was left to install a unit. One concession was made. The auditorium would be air-conditioned by having a ceiling conduit equipped with a huge fan that would blow air over a block of dry ice through the ceiling vents. At the time, ice was cheap and this system was state of the art. However, as the price of ice went up, the system was used less and less. By the time Mr. Thelen became principal, no one wanted to risk turning on a fan that might blow out who knows what from the conduit.

The building is quirky, as are most older schools that have a past—and the quirkiness is part of the charm and ambience. Our country is filled with such schools, some now modernized and some slated for demolition to be replaced by state-of-the-art facilities. Principals lucky enough to be in pre–World War II buildings, however, have schools with a history and uniqueness that their colleagues in new but pre-fab schools lack.

Though the school was not renovated, there were some positive outcomes. To prepare for what was expected to be a major renovation beginning in two years, Mr. Thelen reduced enrollment. This coincided with an influx of money to reduce class size. Even when the project was scrapped, he did not increase enrollment as the average class size had dropped significantly and there were no longer enough classrooms to house additional students.

Mr. Thelen's AP/Organization began a program with his counterpart in another vocational school that trained students for the construction trades. The student crews systematically ripped out all the secluded locker areas and turned them into small offices (unfortunately without windows) or storage areas. These locker areas had been student smoking and tryst places that drew school aides and security agents from more important tasks. The lockers themselves were not secure. On the tour, the assistant principal showed Mr. Thelen how a student using one locker could easily bend away the metal forming the back of the adjacent locker.

With the help of the student organization and Parent Association, the school was able to get the district to install new lockers along the main corridors on each floor of the building. The assistant principal devised a plan for locker distribution so that a student was assigned the same locker for his or her entire stay at the school and was responsible for its "upkeep."

The school had new windows installed, ones that actually opened and did not suddenly crash down like a guillotine upon unsuspecting hands and arms. Since Mr. Thelen retired, many rooms have been air-conditioned to make the required summer programs bearable. Many public spaces in the school are enhanced by permanent murals, the legacy of the art majors of each graduating class.

The above musings are not irrelevant meanderings. Newly assigned assistant principals, chairs, principals, and heads of schools need to explore their buildings and surrounding neighborhoods. Schools drawing students from an immediate residential neighborhood will have one set of issues, while schools drawing students from areas far away will have a different set, such as student absenteeism or lateness because of transportation delays.

Older buildings will have maintenance issues and quirky architectural problems. Ironically, new buildings, given modern and careless construction methods, may need even more repairs—and there will be no school lore pinpointing student hiding places. A school's physical plant and neighborhood have significant impact on instruction.

The principal is responsible for all educational aspects of the school. The physical plant is maintained by the custodial engineer (hereafter referred to as the custodian) and his or her crew. Much has been written about the abuses and inefficiency of the custodians in the public schools. In the experiences of the urban principals who populate these pages, these instances tend to be the exceptions, not the rule. Just as a small percentage of incompetent teachers cause public misgivings about the whole profession, so a minority of poor custodians have unfairly led to all custodians being considered inefficient or negligent.

Some cities and townships have given principals the option of hiring contracted custodial services rather than have an onsite custodian. According to the New York City custodian's union, a significant percentage of principals who opted for a private contractor switched back to having a traditional custodian because they found the level of services provided by the contractors to be poor. It would seem that both the school custodial system and the private contract system have issues and are subject to abuses.

Every school in this country has a custodian of some sort. None of the principals cited in this book worked with a private contractor, so all that follows is based on school leaders' experiences in working with the traditional school custodian. The great advantage of this system is that the person responsible for the physical plant of the school is onsite. School leaders in large urban districts often also have access to regional custodial supervisors who assist the school in arranging for major repairs beyond the job description of the onsite custodian.

Academic Vocational High was a custodian's retirement village, given the Byzantine contract the district had with the union. Custodians received additional compensation depending on the size of the school—its square footage—as well as its type of facilities. A school with athletic fields or swimming pools generated salary stipends.

When a custodian retired, or transferred to another school, other custodians could apply for the vacated position. The applicant with the highest seniority and a satisfactory rating would be awarded the job. As custodians gained seniority, they looked to transfer to bigger schools to increase their compensation. They hoped to retire from a very large school so that all the additional stipends would become part of their pension computation. In other words, the very contract negotiated provided financial incentives for custodians to continually transfer to larger schools, leading to constant turnover, especially in smaller schools.

Mr. Thelen's school, being in midtown Manhattan, had neither athletic fields nor swimming pools, but as a 10-story building with two gyms and a very large auditorium, it had a great deal of square footage. It had two other attractive perks for senior custodians. Its custodial staff had been with the school for many years and took great pride in keeping a beautiful art deco building well maintained. They were self-motivated. Second, the school was well run and the majority of the students took pride in their school, making the job of the custodian easy. As custodians approached retirement age, they waited until this school's custodian retired so they could replace him—hence, Mr. Thelen's nickname for his school, Boca Raton High.

Some custodians Principal Thelen worked with were more active than others, despite pending retirement. Once they realized that their staffs were self-motivating, they tended to allow what always was to continue. Many took advantage of opportunities (also specified in their contracts) to temporarily serve as a custodian in another school awaiting the assignment of a permanent custodian. This process often took months, thereby greatly increasing their salaries and possible pensions, depending upon when they retired.

In most school districts, principals do not negotiate contracts with custodians. Their only concern is the maintenance of their physical plants. With the exception of one custodian, all those assigned to Mr. Thelen did a fine job with such maintenance. If there was any issue, they addressed it. If it was beyond the scope of the ability of the staff, such as an electrical problem requiring a licensed electrician, they filed the appropriate request for services and worked with the district custodial supervisor.

The crew did work beyond contractual requirements as they were often in the school doing overtime for the rentals of the school building. By district policy, renters of school facilities had to pay an hourly rate for custodial help for the entire time of the rental in case a problem developed, such as the lights not going on. In reality the crew was needed to open the building, then clean at the end of the rental and lock the school. The crew used the time between to help with projects that needed addressing around the school such as the painting of classrooms or hallways.

One custodian did nothing and was rarely in the building, although his time card always indicated otherwise. His goal was to get a bigger school in Queens, as he lived on Long Island and would find this commute easier. Many Queens schools, in addition to high square footage, have extensive athletic fields. The following anecdote illustrates a Catch-22 of the entire system.

Each year principals rated their custodians. If a custodian had a poor rating, he would not be considered for a transfer. However, from the principal's standpoint, giving a poor rating insured that a poor custodian remained in the school since actual dismissals of custodians were rare. Mr. Thelen made a deal with his absentee custodian. He would give him a satisfactory rating if the custodian transferred to the first bigger school that came along. Soon, this custodian was gone and his school had another soon-to-be retiree who planned to stay only three years. He was still there when Principal Thelen— and then his successor—retired. He liked the ambience of the school and the self-motivation of his crew so much, he stayed to add a few more pensionable years.

The rating of the poor custodian as satisfactory gave the problem to another school. Mr. Thelen did not make the Byzantine rules, but he used them to insure that *his* school's physical plant continued to be maintained. Different districts will have unique arrangements for the maintenance of their schools. Savvy principals learn how to manipulate district procedures to best maintain their schools.

Excluding contractual issues, the most important part of working with the custodian and his crew is one of respect. With the one exception mentioned above, all the custodians and crew members the principals in this book worked with were dedicated workers who wanted to keep their schools looking and running well. They may not have had college degrees, but they had the mechanical, handyman skills needed to maintain the physical plant.

During his first meeting with newly assigned teachers, Mr. Thelen told his neophytes to be courteous and respectful to the entire custodial staff. Once they liked you, they would help you with anything you needed, from repairing window shades, to rearranging rooms, to completing minor repairs not in the contract. Like the professional staff, they were there to improve the ambience of the school.

Chapter Twelve

Dealing with the Larger Context: The School District, Media, Advisory Boards, and Celebrities

By design, the name of this and the next chapter sound like the title in a standard textbook dealing with an Educational Leadership Constituents Council (ELCC) leadership competency. They describe how the school leader interacts with the larger context outside of the school. This competency is not a top priority of most school leaders. Certainly it occupies a rung below the other areas. It is a weakness of many school leaders, including those cited in this book whose strengths are in the areas of human relations, staff development, and the improvement of instruction. Perhaps this skill improves the longer principals lead as the handling of other priorities becomes easier and there is more time and energy to devote to the larger context.

To some extent, Mr. Chen's less-than-stellar ability in this area stemmed from fear, particularly of "the powers that be" and the media. Mr. Paul, his predecessor as principal of Brooklyn High, had a small plaque made for his office: *Cherish Obscurity*. He left it for Mr. Chen when he retired. His basic philosophy was if "they" don't know you're there—if you don't make waves, if you give "them" what they want and stay out of the newspapers—"they" will leave you alone and you can get on with your job without interference. Mr. Paul was referring to the district, the superintendent, and all "the powers that be." He did well with this philosophy.

When Mr. Chen's principal advised him to apply for the top position at Brooklyn High, he admitted to her that he never had heard of the place, even though the school was less than a mile from the nearby Brooklyn Bridge. Students and parents knew of the school through word of mouth and recommendations from savvy middle school counselors who knew it had a quiet reputation for a strong instructional program and safe environment. But, most teachers looking for jobs only knew of the school as a name on a list of

Brooklyn high schools, neither famous like Brooklyn Tech nor infamous as some other schools—just a mid-sized school tucked into a residential block in the Park Slope section of the borough.

Part of a school leader's job is not creating problems for the district. Another is giving the district the statistics they are looking for while at the same time educating children. Avoiding negative press is another task. This was not much of an issue for Mr. Chen. Even the media didn't seem to know his school existed. He made sure he did nothing to draw their attention.

For example, his predecessor told him that the media monitor all 911 emergency calls, whether to ask for police help or for an ambulance for a sick or injured student or staff member. Call 911, and it was possible a news vehicle would be outside the school looking for a story. Mr. Chen did not use 911. He called his local precinct directly when he needed help, using the always-open line of his liaison sergeant. He called a nearby hospital with its own ambulance service when there was a medical emergency.

Mr. Paul had been adamant about avoiding the news media. Midway through his principalship, he gave a lengthy interview to an apparently interested and competent reporter. The next day, about 10 seconds of his 10-minute interview was used in a news report. It was taken out of context and led the viewer to believe the exact opposite of what Mr. Paul meant to convey. Mr. Paul was not wrong. Mr. Chen knew how the news media could take a positive story and turn it on its head. Good news is not news, except for human-interest fillers.

Each year, the district, with the cooperation of a private support organization, Pencil Inc., sponsored a "Principal for a Day" event. Pencil Inc. tried to pair a business executive or celebrity with a school, making him or her the school's "principal for a day," shadowing the real principal, meeting students and staff, perhaps making a presentation or teaching a class. Pencil Inc. and the district hoped that the executive or celebrity would better understand how schools work, explain this to their contacts, and, perhaps, offer scholarships or other material supports.

Mr. Thelen at his academic-vocational school often had "principals" from the apparel industry: fashion designers, fashion house mangers, modeling agency representatives, department store executives, and a *Vanity Fair* executive vice president. He usually fared well with his principals for a day. The *Vanity Fair* executive, for example, encouraged all her contacts to donate excess fabric to the school, creating a support network that continued for many years.

Not all schools fared as well. One year, a middle school had a local news reporter as its principal for a day. There was an incident at the school, the police were called, and a student was arrested. The reporter, who was supposed to provide a positive story on the school and the principal-for-a-day initiative, instead followed the student to the precinct and reported on the untoward incident and the treatment of the child at the police station.

Schools are fair game for the media. Any story in which children can be portrayed as victims makes good news. The swine (H1N1) flu scare was in full swing in spring 2009. The actual outbreak was centered in one parochial high school in Queens whose students had contracted the illness in Mexico during the spring recess. Rightly, this school was closed for several days. However, a few instances of minor undiagnosed illnesses in public schools, predominantly in Queens, and then spreading to the rest of the city, led to several school closings.

The media kept reporting on the illnesses, parents afraid to send their children to school and the few H1N1 related deaths. No mention was made of the fact that 30,000 people nationwide die of complications of the flu in any given year. In over-reporting the story, the media created an atmosphere of panic among parents, students, and even staff. Reporters made sure to interview terrified parents who would not send their children to school. Schools were unnecessarily closed. Thousands of students were kept home and lost instructional time.

One of Mr. Chen's colleagues looked at the schools that were closed in Queens. Most were in close proximity to a major shopping mall where teens, pre-teens, and children with their parents frequently shopped. No one suggested shutting down the mall to stop the spread of the disease.

The media salivate at any allegations of sexual misconduct or teacher abuse of power. Such incidents, involving a minute percentage of educators, make headlines that cast a shadow over the rest of the dedicated professionals who labor day in and day out. No wonder a school leader may want to *Cherish Obscurity*. Having said this, we will now look at experiences in which school leaders, exerting some control, interacted positively with the "larger context." The next chapter will explore other aspects of the "larger context" over which school leaders have little control and less input.

The context can never be larger than the 9/11 terrorist attack on the World Trade Center. Mr. Thelen's Academic Vocational High is fewer than two miles north of the World Trade Center. The towers could be clearly seen from the upper floors of the school. September 11, 2001, was a beautifully clear day. The gym teachers took their students out of the warm, un-air-conditioned gym to this vertical school's rooftop "playground" for running exercises. These students saw the planes hit the towers, as did students in classrooms on the upper stories of the south side of the building, as did Mr. Thelen from the small balcony outside his office.

The best information he received came from a local all-news radio station. He used the school's intercom to keep the school community informed of what was happening and to ask all students and staff to stay in their classrooms and continue with the normal school day. It was safer to stay in place than to go into an uncertain city where all public transportation had been shut down. Mr. Thelen was all over the school, stopping into as many rooms as possible to calm students. He was joined by the entire supervisory staff.

Without him even directing them, his staff went to work. Marcia, AP/Student Support Services, and her guidance department organized the auditorium into a counseling area and parent pickup center. Mike, AP/Security, worked with the local precinct and transit authority to determine when public transportation would be available. He arranged for box dinners and cots to be set up in case some students or staff could not get home. Teachers allowed students to share their fears and did all they could to maintain some semblance of calm. Eileen, Mr. Thelen's secretary, set up the principal's office as a "command post."

There is no way to train staff for an extraordinary emergency. A school leader trusts that past training will allow teachers and administrators alike to do the right thing. In many ways, 9/11 was this staff's finest hour. There was little panic. There was an organized system for parents to pick up their children. Students who felt they could travel were given the latest information on which trains were running and directed to return to the school if these trains were again halted. Students who wanted to stay in the school and wait for their parents were welcome to do so. Teachers and administrators volunteered to stay to supervise. Mr. Thelen was one of the last to leave at about 8:30. There were no students left in the school and no more were returning as public transportation was again operating.

His school community was almost unscathed. No child lost a parent, although there were the usual stories of close calls. Some staff members lost friends and acquaintances. There was one major tragedy: a staff member lost her fiancé—he was in the second tower talking to her and assuring her that he would be all right when the phone went dead. Only a few weeks earlier, many teachers in her department had been to their engagement party.

The guidance staff set up group and individual counseling sessions for staff and students to help them deal with the aftermath of 9/11. Volunteer staff members came in on days the school was closed to plan special lessons for the children.

The real story of the "larger context" for Mr. Thelen's school came after the tragedy of 9/11. Academic Vocational High became a shelter school, its gym used to shelter people displaced by the destruction. On paper, this sounds heroic. In actuality, most of those sheltered were street people from lower Manhattan who saw this as an opportunity for free meals and a safe place to sleep—and an opportunity for thievery. The AP/Security was diligent in locking down everything and working with the custodian, the Red Cross, and city agencies to protect the school while also serving the needs of truly displaced people. As a result, there were few problems.

Several schools in lower Manhattan were close to Ground Zero. They suffered severe damage and needed to be thoroughly cleansed of hazardous materials. While this was done, the students needed to be educated. About one week after the terrorist attack, Mr. Thelen was told that another school would be housed in his building. The district plan called for Academic Vocational High students to report an hour early, have shortened periods, and be dismissed by 1:00. The displaced students would then begin a late school session of similarly shortened periods.

Mr. Thelen devised an alternative plan to maintain full-length classes by using an overlapping schedule that maximized classroom use during his students' four lunch periods (when about one-fourth of the classrooms were empty). He devised the following schedule, approved by the district.

Academic Vocational High began and ended on its regular schedule. All periods were full length. The visiting school, instead of being on a 1:30 to 6:30 schedule, began at 10:35 and ended at 5:15. All periods were full length. Academic Vocational High had about 1,600 students at the time; the visiting school, about 500, making this type of schedule possible.

This worked programmatically, but Mr. Thelen failed to anticipate two major problems. First, the students and staff of the visiting school had been badly traumatized. They had been adjacent to Ground Zero and were evacuated on boats across the Hudson River. They saw the terror up close. Their staff suffered significant losses of family and friends. Second, as a small school, it had a different ambience and approach to discipline. In Mr. Thel-

Academic Vocational High School	Period Begins	Visiting High School
Period 1	8:15	(no classes)
Period 2	9:00	(no classes)
Period 3	9:45	(no classes)
Period 4 (LUNCH - ¼ of classrooms free)	10:35	Period 1
Period 5 (LUNCH - ¼ of classrooms free)	11:20	Period 2
Period 6 (LUNCH - ¼ of classrooms free)	12:05	Period 3
Period 7 (LUNCH - ¼ of classrooms free)	12:50	Period 4
Period 8 (all classrooms in use)	1:35	Period 5 (Lunch for all students)
Period 9 (half of classrooms free)	2:20	Period 6
	3:05	Period 7 (Gyms free for use)
	3:50	Period 8 (One gym free for use)
	4:30	Period 9 (If needed)

Figure 12.1. Overlapping Class Schedule.

en's large school, discipline was impersonal, stressing that the rules were the same for all regardless of circumstance. In the small visiting school, discipline was personalized and less rigid. These combined issues led to some contention over the next five months.

The weekend before the merger was to begin, Mr. Thelen's programming staff volunteered to report to the school to rearrange Academic Vocational High's room assignments so that the visiting staff would not be haphazardly assigned to vacant rooms and wind up with five classes in five different rooms. However, the programming staff of the visiting school said they could not make it. Without their input, nothing could be done. In retrospect, they just needed a break from the horror they had witnessed; however, at the time, it seemed to Mr. Thelen that they were missing an opportunity to make life easier for their teachers.

So, at the beginning several visiting teachers had five rooms. Academic Vocational High teachers, working one on one, made arrangements to switch rooms and the programming staff assisted in altering the master program to allow this. It took time, but most visiting teachers ended up with fewer room assignments.

Discipline was a more contentious issue. Looking back today, Mr. Thelen realizes that his security team should have met with the visiting school's team to make it clear that in his building, Academic Vocational High discipline rules would be followed—though, this strategy may in itself have led to strife with a school struggling to maintain its identity in a foreign building. There were incidents where Mr. Thelen's deans stopped visiting students in the hall between periods and brought them to their own school's makeshift office, only to see the students immediately allowed to go to class. The deans felt their authority undermined, as their own students would have been under house suspension until their parents came to the school for a conference.

Sometimes, the deans brought the visiting students to their own office, only to face the ire of their counterparts who felt their authority was being usurped. The overlapping schedules saved instructional time but promoted inter-school tension, heightened by the trauma of the events of 9/11.

Overall, such incidents were just irritating exceptions. The teachers of both schools worked well together, as did most of the students. Joint school patrols alleviated some of the tension. Every period, staff from both schools patrolled the halls together. Mr. Thelen himself patrolled one period a day with an administrator from the visiting school. This show of cooperation among adults had a positive effect on students.

Both schools survived and both rejoiced when the visitors triumphantly marched back to their cleaned and refurbished school at the end of the fall semester. At the annual supervisory award ceremony, an assistant principal from each school received an award for working together through the crises. In June, Academic Vocational High students posted the highest test statistics the school had every achieved.

Mr. Thelen's Academic Vocational High had an industry Vocational Advisory Board (VAB). It was established in the 1930's when the school was chartered so that representatives of the apparel industries could overview and monitor the school's occupational programs. Such boards were required for all vocational programs in the district. During his early years as principal, Mr. Thelen did not pay enough attention to this valuable resource as he focused on staff development, curriculum changes, and severe budget cuts.

For the most part, the VAB Mr. Thelen inherited was a social club for long-time members who were past giants of an industry that was diminishing as more and more garment construction was being outsourced to foreign countries. As a result, he often had to contend with the old ideas of members as he tried to initiate major curriculum changes reducing occupational coursework as academic requirements increased. Many old-timers (there were several octogenarians and nonagenarians on the committee) and some graduates of the school decried this change, still seeing an industry in need of sewing machine operators.

Newer members realized that the future of the school lay in training students for higher-level positions and giving them entry-level skills for post-secondary programs in schools like the Fashion Institute of Technology or Parsons The New School for Design. In areas of curriculum, the VAB had no real authority. The state and district determined the academic requirements that principals had to implement. Mr. Thelen could only try to explain what he had to do.

A major portion of the VAB's time was spent planning an annual dinner dance to raise scholarship money for students. This was more of a social affair for members and their friends and, after expenses, raised only enough of money to maintain a modest program. It also sometimes brought new members onto the committee and, through careful selection of honorees, new supporters of school programs.

For years, Mr. Thelen tried unsuccessfully to substitute a cocktail reception at the school's spring fashion show. He felt this would bring potential supporters into the school itself (the dinner dance was always held at some other venue) to see the best work of the students. With minimal overhead costs, elicited donations would be almost total profit. His successor as principal succeeded where he failed. Mr. Thelen would like to think that some of the newer VAB members who joined while he was principal became the cadre who supported this change, but it is more likely that his successor was better able to work with this "larger context."

The establishment of an annual Career College Fair was one of his successes. This was the brainchild of the VAB chair, a Bloomingdale's executive. In addition to the fair's providing a day of information on careers and colleges for students, several presenters went on to become supporters of the school and VAB members.

Looking back, Mr. Thelen feels that if he were to become a principal today, he would try to give more time and attention to such an advisory board.

The people on it are already supporters of the school, predisposed to give time, talent, and sometimes money. They have multiple contacts from their professional lives, all potential school supporters.

Mr. Thelen's first experience with a single corporation involved a grant program with the Fashion House Foundation which he inherited when he became principal. This foundation wanted to contribute to the education of children and found Academic Vocational High to be a natural venue for their grant. One of his first tasks on becoming principal was to establish a task force to work with the grant administrator to create a program for the students of his school.

At this point, Mr. Thelen was not adept at running productive meetings. Fortunately, the foundation representative, Ms. Melody, was. She saw that most of the issues the different members of the school community were targeting related to the achievement of the incoming students. Once she presented this as a focus, the committee was able to come up with concrete suggestions for foundation money, creating supports for these students.

The main funding piece was the use of grant money to reward ninth (and later tenth) year students who passed all their classes with a Fashion House Foundation Achievement Gift Certificate redeemable for merchandise at the school store. This appealed to the funding source on several levels. First, it encouraged students to pass all their classes, establishing a pattern of success that would continue throughout their high school careers. Second, it created customers for the store, a classroom laboratory for merchandising majors. Because of the influx of these customers, students would have more experiences managing, marketing, and selecting items to sell and actually purchasing items from suppliers. Third, it provided the students receiving awards a way to purchase supplies and materials they might need in their occupational classes.

Mr. Thelen found out that any monetary grant from a funding source usually requires "in kind" support from the school. The school designed and duplicated the award certificates. The principal personally awarded the certificates to the students each marking period. He compiled and monitored pass/fail statistics to document the efficacy of the program and made sure the books balanced when he submitted invoices to the foundation. Other aspects of the focus on ninth year students, described in chapter 8, required no monetary support, such as changes in the orientation of incoming ninth graders, the assignment of their teachers, and the programming of students.

Mr. Thelen likes to tell a humorous anecdote related to the original grant proposal he submitted. As a new principal, he was not yet adept at planning ahead and getting long-term projects done long before the due date. He now had less than two weeks to the proposal submission deadline when he fell victim to an inner ear infection that affected his balance. After school on Friday, he went to a "Doc in a Box" and was given Sudafed. The medication acted as an "upper" on his system and he couldn't sleep all weekend. He spent day and night word processing the proposal. By Monday, it was done and he was exhausted. He went to a good ear, nose, and throat doctor, who thought the whole incident humorous as he explained that Sudafed affects some people that way. Mr. Thelen never took this medication again.

The grant was renewed several times, but after about eight years, the focus of the foundation shifted from education to health issues and the monetary support for the program came to an end. Fortunately, a member of the VAB was able to secure an alternate funding source. This time, no formal proposal was needed, as it was a contribution to the school's VAB Scholarship Fund. After this emergency influx of funds, the VAB itself shifted its scholarship focus, formally only on upperclassman, to include funding the incentive program for incoming students.

As mentioned, Principal for a Day was a district initiative that paired a business leader or celebrity with a principal so that the former could learn firsthand about the positives of education in a New York City school. It is an excellent program for raising the awareness of the movers and shakers in the city and sometimes it leads to special support for the school. School districts around the country sponsor similar programs. Celebrity graduates sometimes visit their old schools to address and encourage students. All special visitors mean more work for school leaders.

Principal for a Day certainly led to more work for Mr. Chen and his leadership staff at Brooklyn High. They met to discuss how to plan the day for their corporate or celebrity principal. They agreed to include several components:

- An introductory breakfast with students from different grade levels. The students would make formal presentations on their classes and also respond to the guest's questions.
- A tour of the school and, if the guest wished, visits to classes and even short presentations within these classes. Mr. Chen contacted the visitor in

advance to see if he or she wanted something more, such as an auditorium presentation. None did, although several wanted to "teach" or at least speak with students in specific classes.
- A luncheon with the cabinet and officers of the Parent Association, where questions could be answered from a different point of view.
- A meeting with students on the school newspaper and yearbook to allow for articles to be written and photographs taken.
- And finally, an exit meeting with Mr. Chen to see if anything more could come out of this visit.

This plan worked very well. The only refinement later made was to make the school tour more inclusive. The original tour plan tended to be overladen with honors classes and did not show the excellent professional work being done by students of all levels and abilities. School leaders expecting celebrity visitors might find the above plan adaptable to their needs.

It still amazes Mr. Chen and his colleagues how little the general public—and this includes the principals for a day—know about education. They see headlines about problems, but know little of the successes and the daily struggles faced by both staff and students. In his school, he felt all visitors came away with a positive feeling about education, students, and teachers.

Mr. Thelen used a similar plan, with more emphasis on visits to vocational classrooms. His principals for a day, often from the apparel industry, were impressed. Unfortunately, this did not always translate into material support for the school.

An example is the Big Fashion Name who actually came to Mr. Thelen's school twice because he liked his first stint as Principal for a Day so much. Perhaps it was the near adoration of the students that drew him back. He was personable. His classroom presentation on his career and the importance of a good general education was excellent. However, when it came to any support, even a single scholarship in his name, he would always say just call my secretary and she'll set it up. Well, she was never there and when she was, she had no authority or had to speak with so and so or do whatever—and would get back to the school. She never did. The cost of one of Big Fashion Name's newspaper ads could have financed a continuing scholarship for a graduate, but nothing ever came of his visits.

Mr. Thelen learned that the real movers and shakers in the apparel industry were not always the big names. J. P. was an executive vice president at *Vanity Fair* when she visited the school. She was amazed at the talents of the students and distraught by the lack of fabric they had to work with, particularly for lingerie and swimwear. In her position, she bought fabric for her company. A simple hint that a donation to the high school would be appreciated often led to donations of fine fabrics for the students. When a company makes such a donation once, it tends to continue to do so every year. For example, the Underfashion Club, a charitable arm of the lingerie industry, financed a yearly scholarship for a student going to the Fashion Institute of Technology.

Ms. Valletta hosted a celebrity who was interested in her school's theater program. Actor Tony Randall was a major supporter of an off-Broadway theater not far from Manhattan High. Ms. Rouge and her drama club often received free tickets to his shows. However, knowing that what is free is not always valued, she had students "pay" five dollars for the ticket (worth far more). The money was presented at the theater as a donation for Actors Equity Fights AIDS.

Mr. Randall was most impressed by this. At the end of several productions, he and actors from the show came out on stage to speak with the students. They enjoyed interacting with them and answering their perceptive questions (Ms. Rouge was very good at preparing students for such events). He wanted to learn more about their school near his theater and requested to be the school's Principal for a Day.

He was terrific. Even though most students had never heard of him, they were thrilled by his humor and genuine interest in their education. Toward the end of his visit, he ran into a student who had presented at the breakfast meeting and greeted her by name. She said, "You remember me!" His response, "Of course, that's part of my job as an actor." While on the school tour, an older staff member said that he remembered him from those pictures he made with Doris Day—"How many did you make with her?" His deadpan response: "Two—two too many."

The school did not get monetary support from Mr. Randall as all his spare change was going into the struggling theater. But, the students were given many more free tickets to productions.

In large districts such as New York City, the superintendent or even the chancellor may bring the larger context to the school. Larry Woodward was a New York City Department of Education survivor. Chancellors changed every two to five years, but Larry was always connected with his office in one way or another, usually as a troubleshooter and problem solver. He was a member of the Level II selection committee that interviewed Mr. Thelen when he was seeking the principal's job.

Larry called Mr. Thelen shortly after he became principal. The AIDS epidemic was now at its peak and the New York State Department of Education had mandated that AIDS prevention lessons be taught in all public schools. Most lessons were mandated, but parents could opt out their children from a lesson on the use of contraceptives. Each school had to submit a plan detailing how the lessons would be taught and what procedure would be established to keep track of the parental opt out.

The plan submitted by Mr. Thelen's staff was well received by the district office. To minimize impact on the curriculum in each subject area, their plan dispersed the lessons taught into different recitation classes. In social studies, the history of epidemics in general and AIDS in particular was taught. In English, students discussed the impact of the epidemic on their neighborhoods or their own families, leading to discussions and essays on their fears about the disease. In science, students were taught about the biology of the epidemic. The mandated lesson on abstinence and preventing the spread of AIDS was taught in the health class, as was the controversial "opt out" lesson on the use of contraceptives. Ms. Bess Liu, the designated AIDS Education Coordinator for the school, taught these health classes.

An affiliate of a national television network was doing a story on the school system's response to the epidemic and asked the district for permission to film a lesson in progress—of course, the optional one on the use of contraceptives. The reporter also wanted to interview a teacher and some students. Larry was asked by the district to designate a school and he chose Mr. Thelen's high school located in midtown Manhattan, near the network's home base. He called to ask Mr. Thelen if he would accept this task. This was a polite formality as the principal had no choice.

Mr. Thelen and his staff did all the preliminary work needed, getting releases from the parents of the students in the class to allow filming and, for some students, individual interviews. Ms. Liu also completed a release form. Administrative staff cordoned off the area where the film crew would be working to minimize the impact on the school day.

Word of the filming leaked out and conservative organizations totally opposed to any AIDS prevention program picketed outside. The local police made sure they were not blocking entry to the school and the students ignored the fuss as they entered. The piece that aired that night was well balanced and presented all the facts correctly. Ms. Liu proved to be an excellent spokesperson on the need for such instruction to save the lives of children.

An unanticipated consequence taught Mr. Thelen a lesson for future dealings with the media. Once a story is filmed, all footage belongs to the contracted company. Once they have a release to use it, they can use the piece as they wish, even selling it to other markets. For the next few years, Ms. Liu found herself a poster teacher for AIDS prevention, with parts of the segment appearing in media markets around the country and her still photo in a national magazine. Mr. Thelen contacted Larry who connected him with the district's legal office. He found out there nothing could be done to stop this continued use of the footage. It was allowed under the standard film release form used by the district.

Over the years, Mr. Thelen had other calls from Larry and always accommodated his requests. While he had no choice, he knew that graciously accepting such requests and doing his best to make sure everything went well would put a "plus" in his column. If he ever had a future need, he would be able to call in a favor or two. *Always be owed more favors than you owe to others* is a good rule for school leaders.

One call concerned the accessibility of school programs, still a national and local issue. Many specialized schools, built decades ago, are not handicapped accessible. Groups representing children with physical challenges lobbied the district to correct this. Schools were made more accessible. As Mr. Thelen's school already had student elevators, it was one of the first buildings to receive modifications. A ramp was added to the main entrance. A wheelchair section was added to the auditorium and a removable ramp attached to the back of the stage to make it accessible to physically challenged students or staff for graduation ceremonies and other events.

The local NBC news station wanted to do a story on how schools were becoming more accessible and Larry gave Mr. Thelen a call. The principal was honest with him. The modifications were window dressing. Even before they were made, the few students with physical challenges had no difficulty navigating the school and doing well in some vocational concentrations. However, those wanting to major in fashion design would still find the program inaccessible. Larry told Mr. Thelen to be honest with the reporter.

The principal personally showed the reporter the modifications made and then took her to a fashion design room with its circa 1940's foot-treadle sewing machines, totally inaccessible to any child in a wheelchair. The final story was balanced, but it was clear the school—and probably many other older schools with certain occupational concentrations—had a way to go to make all programs accessible. The school still has the same 1940's machines today.

As with the Principal for a Day program, sometimes, the "larger context" sent to a school by the district or superintendent involves celebrity visitors. In the 1990's, it was common for students to "trick or treat" for contributions to UNICEF. The New York City public schools were involved in this effort to raise money for the poor children of developing nations.

The Manhattan High School superintendent received a call from a representative of UNICEF. The organization wanted to kick off that year's campaign in a public school by having the chairperson of UNICEF and their spokesperson, supermodel Vendela (who had once graced the cover of a *Sports Illustrated* swimsuit issue), visit a school and speak with students. Steve Greenstreet, the superintendent's executive assistant, immediately connected a supermodel with Mr. Thelen's apparel-oriented school and again Mr. Thelen received a call.

This was one of those times when it's good to be the principal. By this time, he and his staff were adept at handling celebrities and everything went smoothly to the satisfaction of all parties. After the photo shoot, while the UNICEF chairperson was talking with the news media, Vendela asked if she could rest a few minutes in Mr. Thelen's private office, saying she needed a break. What could a principal say? His wife never lets him forget that he was alone with a supermodel—and how he later received a personal thank-you card for his hospitality. He was the envy of every male principal in the borough.

Mr. Thelen never mentioned that in their conversation, Vendela explained how she was glad she was getting out of the modeling business and going home to her native Sweden to marry her fiancé and become a normal person.

Also in the 1990's, an arts organization in New York City, supported by substantial contributions, realized that many art works in New York's public buildings, particularly its schools, were badly deteriorating from lack of maintenance. They began a campaign to save the public art of the city. As noted, Mr. Thelen's auditorium is flanked on both sides by two magnificent

174   *Chapter Twelve*

murals done as a WPA project when the school was built. Since the school had been well run since its inception, there was no graffiti on these art works and they had not been vandalized. But they were in great need of a cleaning.

Because the work involved was relatively minor, these murals were among the first art works in a city school to be restored. The principal and staff were amazed to see the brilliance of the colors after the cleaning. There was a special ceremony to recognize the work of the charitable groups involved as well as the artist who had created the murals. As this was an evening event, it was easy to plan for and brought positive press to the school, as well as then-mayor David Dinkins, his wife, descendants of the artist, and leaders of arts organizations in the city.

In an old yearbook, Mr. Thelen found a description of the murals, written in the inflated language of a bygone era. The anonymous author (the painter?) explained the symbolism and named the people depicted. Using this document and some of the lore handed down to him by his predecessor, Mr. Thelen created a flyer on the landmark murals and included portions in his teacher and student handbooks. The history and artifacts of a school are important.

"The larger context" may involve a school leader after retirement. Two years after he retired, Mr. Thelen and his wife were shopping for their daughter's wedding trousseau in a premier department store. As the purchases were being processed, the sales representative's cell phone rang. She answered the call. As she spoke, she moved away from the sale's desk as Mr. Thelen and his wife waited. A floor manager walked by. She could not but help see all this, but said nothing. After a few minutes, the sales representative continued to handle the purchases, still talking on the phone. After she finished her call, she completed the sale.

The Thelens were aghast. He wrote a letter to the manager of the store about his representative's poor service and rudeness. In the letter, he mentioned that he was a former high school principal. He added that his students were taught how to treat customers and would never have been so inattentive to their needs.

To his surprise, he received a response: an apology, a gift certificate for lunch at the store's restaurant, and an offer to work with the high school. He passed along the contact information to the AP/Marketing of his former school so she could follow up. He thought that would be the last he heard of this as businesspeople and fashionistas often make offers to help, but few follow up.

As he was reading the December 2009 issue of the *CSA Newsletter* (the official publication of the Council of School Supervisors and Administrators, the principal and assistant principal's union), he saw an article about his former school. Twenty-eight junior art majors at the school had participated in a competition sponsored by an Italian outerwear manufacturer. In cooperation with this same department store, limited editions of student-designed merchandise ("prototypes" for possible future products) would be sold there, and three windows of the store would be devoted to displaying the student-designed products. Fifteen percent of the sales would be donated to the school to give scholarship money to each of the students involved in the designs. Mr. Thelen wondered if this program was a result of his 2004 letter.

Chapter Thirteen

Dealing with the Larger Context: Politics, Parents, and Panaceas

Political action has not been mentioned much in this book. One could be generous and say that politicians do not understand education and that given all their other priorities, don't listen when educators speak with them. Most educators are more cynical: Politicians only care about education if it suits their political agendas and gets them reelected. Our democracy, based on electing representatives who carry out the will of the people and make decisions that will benefit the country, has devolved into a group of professional politicians whose main cares are building personal power bases and staying in office. Do they want an educated populace that can astutely see through political rhetoric, discern half-truths, and identify demagogues who promote personal agendas over the good of the people?

These same politicians always point to the "better" education children receive in European countries or Japan. These countries have national exams which are real tests of achievement. Educators may wonder: If these politicos think these other educational systems are so great, why not have such mandatory national exams in the United States? Of course they know the answer. It would be political suicide for any politician from a state which has a poor educational system. Many educators do not accept the premise that other nations have better educational systems nor do they feel high stakes exams that lead to national adolescent anxiety are the best way to evaluate achievement.

Let's look at what the politicians do when they get involved in education. No Child Left Behind was supposed to raise the bar for all students and increase the accountability of teachers, school leaders, and school districts by requiring that all students and schools meet certain benchmarks. Standardized tests determined whether these benchmarks were reached, creating an entire industry for book and test publishers and private tutorial services.

Each state was left to determine its own test. What one state considered high achievement might be considered near-illiteracy by another. A great deal of money was made by publishers, but education did not improve. Teachers were forced to reduce real instruction in favor of test prep. Students were taught how to pass required exams but far less about critical thinking or the joy of learning. One may wonder how many of the politicians who pushed No Child Left Behind had interests in test and text publishing.

As he left office, President Eisenhower warned the country about the perils of the "military-industrial complex." Today, we need to be wary of a new danger: the "political-statistical-test complex."

In New York City, Mike Bloomberg mounted a campaign based on the promise to improve education in the city. He wanted his tenure as mayor to be judged by how well he did this. He claims he succeeded. His television re-election campaign in 2009 heavily stressed that New York City schools were better solely because of his leadership and implied that before him, teachers and school leaders did nothing and students learned little. What an insult to the thousands of dedicated professionals who spent their pre-Bloomberg careers teaching the children of New York City!

If the truth be told, his great successes are all smoke and mirrors. Has the high school graduation rate gone up? Yes, but much of this is due to the "credit recovery" system he and Chancellor Joel Klein instituted, allowing schools to determine their own methods for giving students make-up work, which ranged from short reports to showing up for a few days in the summer to real attempts at helping failing students. The *New York Times* periodically ran a few exposés about the abuses. The Department of Education responded that these were the exception, not the rule, and issued revised guidelines, but little changed with the educational void called "credit recovery."

The mayor defended credit recovery. If this system was so flawed, how could students pass the required state exit exams? From time immemorial, high school students in New York State have had to pass Regents exams in various subject areas. For a long while, those not academically gifted could pass the less-rigorous Regents Competency Tests (RCTs) to graduate from high school. The RCTs were phased out and the new Regents exams phased in, with a "local" passing grade of 55 percent during a long transition period, and then with a required Regents passing grade of 65 percent for all.

During and after this transition period, the statewide passing percentage on the Regents exams remained relatively constant for all exams, about 90 percent. The newly formatted standardized exams put greater emphasis on critical thinking rather than rote memory. However, they are marked on a steep curve to guarantee a certain passing percentage. Math teachers, who enjoy such statistical analysis, know that a student who learns about 30 percent of the curriculum can pass the required mathematics Regents exam because of this curve.

The New York State Board of Regents knows the score. Property values in the districts of state congressional members go up or down based on the test scores in each district. If any subgroup (minority) has a passing percentage significantly lower than the overall passing percentage, there would be political repercussions. So, the Board of Regents created excellent examinations and then neutralized them by using skewed rating systems.

High school students passed the required exams, but are these curved passing grades valid? The mayor and chancellor think so and are adding district tests for students in more grade levels, taking away significant time from real instruction as teachers and school leaders come to understand that "accountability" means training students to get higher test scores. As this is being written, the state, under pressure, has recalibrated scores for standardized exams in the elementary schools, leading to significantly lower passing rates and thousands more students being held back a grade.

Mayor Bloomberg and the New York State Board of Regents are a microcosm of the testing obsession rampant in this entire country. How effective is all this testing? About half the people in the United States of America, the leader of the free world, do not accept the fact of evolution. This speaks reams about our educational system and the failure of our testing mania to teach students to think critically.

The politicians themselves are another sad result of our educational system. In a school system which provides students with a true education, children would graduate with a set of ethical values, would value service to their country and some would become politicians dedicated to their constituencies and the welfare of the nation, not the welfare of themselves.

The above segment on the politicizing of education represents an area within the larger context beyond the influence of school leaders. Organizations of educators often address issues that impact children but their professional voices are drowned by the rhetoric of politicians. The remainder of this section deals with other issues that school leaders discuss among themselves to vent their frustrations.

Let's start big: This nation needs to have its values adjusted. Teaching is a noble and honorable profession. There are tens of thousands of master teachers. They take responsibility for the maturation of the minds and hearts of hundreds of children during their careers. These master teachers are national treasures. They do far more good with their lives than any American Idol, Survivor, pro athlete, pop artist, or movie star.

Yet, in 2011 dollars, these professionals will earn between 2 and 2.5 million dollars over a 30-year career. Not millions for one album or one season or one movie. They will not be honored with an academy award or platinum album or accolades from millions of text voting fans. They will not become Facebook or Twitter personalities. They will quietly and professionally prepare the next generation of Americans. Is there something wrong with our values?

On the flip side, professional organizations have a responsibility to police their members. Unions have a responsibility to protect their members, even those who do not warrant it. Teaching organizations and unions are therefore schizophrenic. If teaching is to become valued as a profession so the tens of thousands of master teachers can receive the salaries and accolades they are due, the profession needs to rid itself of the small minority of teachers and school leaders who are incompetent or just don't care. There is no honor in protecting them. Doing so diminishes the profession.

"Parents are our partners" is a catchphrase of education. And yet, many of the issues schools face are caused by parents, perhaps the largest context over which school leaders have little control.

Parents need to raise their children to love reading and learning, to know how to socialize with peers and adults, to take responsibility for their actions. This cannot be done with a television serving as a permanent babysitter or a computer terminal in the nursery. Most children's futures are indelibly stamped by the early years of their lives, before they even enter school. If a five-year-old cannot be controlled by his or her parents, how can these parents expect teachers to do so?

Parents need to read to their children and play with their children. They need to find ample opportunities for them to socialize with other children. They need to understand that contrived play dates are not real play. They need to teach them right from wrong. They need to teach their children personal responsibility and the consequences for misbehavior in social situations. Teachers are not there these first years and cannot be responsible for the lack of parenting.

Parents also need to guard children from the pitfalls of the electronic age and the omnipresence of the computer monitor, the iPod, the Blackberry, and the cell phone. There is a life without all of these accoutrements. They need to support the schools by limiting time in front of the monitor; providing children with a quiet place to read, study, and do homework; activating parental controls on computers; and, finally, making it very clear that cell phones must be turned off in school at all times. Sad to say, often the most egregious violators of cell-phone use in schools are the parents, themselves slaves of this electronic age, who feel they must call their children at school for the most mundane reasons.

Parents must also convey the message that education is a preparation for life. The school is the venue where futures are fashioned. Most principals cannot count the number of parents who call to ask that their children be excused from school so they can begin Thanksgiving, Christmas, President's Week, spring recess, or summer vacation early—or return from them late.

The principals cited in this book always said *No!* The children would have to make up all the work and, if they missed any exams, would have to work this out with their teachers. Absence due to extended vacations cannot be excused. Much of this has to do with reducing traveling expenses, with which we can all sympathize. However, children in this country have about 200 school days per year, far fewer than in other industrialized nations. Each day is important. What message about the value of education do parents send to their children when they ask for more days off for whatever reason? What message do they send when they keep children home because it is too cold or too hot or little Tommy has an upset tummy?

School is serious business. It is preparation for life and the world of work. The habits established during the school years will impact the work ethic of future adults. Is it any wonder that employers today bemoan the poor work habits of young people?

Finally, if parents are to convey the message that school is serious business, they can do so by dressing children appropriately. The older the child gets, the more his or her dress should reflect a serious mentality. Street wear, obscene t-shirts, baggy pants hanging down below the underwear, and provocative dress emulating the latest pop star are all inappropriate for school. The school uniform movement is a strategy to combat this problem. Parents save money that would have been spent on fad clothes, and appropriate dress is insured. And yet, some parents in schools with such a uniform dress code opt their children out of the program, citing individual freedom.

Teachers, the adult role models of appropriate dress and behavior, also need to dress for serious business. Having children and teachers dress more appropriately for the serious business of school would reduce discipline problems significantly.

Sometimes, the larger context takes the form of overadvocacy. All children are special needs children. All are unique. All are born beautiful, with talents and deficits. However, in today's world we have blurred the line between uniqueness and clinically proven special needs. Part of this is a response to many decades when children with clinically proven needs were not given the proper education. The education pendulum always swings from one extreme to the other. Clouding this educational issue is the current tendency of physicians to overdiagnose and overmedicate, often because patients, having been inundated with medically themed television programs and commercials, demand medication for every perceived health problem.

Something is wrong when we forget that not all uniqueness requires clinical interventions. Some children just grow faster than others; some read more quickly; some have greater manual dexterity earlier. Many parents and educators insist on clinical testing when a child is a few months behind the average reader, but no one thinks it a problem if he or she cannot play a musical instrument. We have homogenized children instead of celebrating their diversity. The question is not "Why can't Johnny read?" but "Why can't Johnny read at the prescribed level for the average four-year-and-three-month-old?" Our master teachers have understood the uniqueness and diversity of children from the days of the one-room schoolhouse, but today it is cause for alarming parents and calling in the experts.

Is the fact that so many children are now classified with a variety of special needs akin to the fact that half of the people in this country are considered to have high blood pressure? Who determines the norm? Or, perhaps a better question, who makes money from the norm? Let's be honest. There is a whole industry now devoted to homogenizing children so that they all read, write, and do math at the same level at the same time. The system is abused when parents in affluent communities use personal psychologists to have their children diagnosed with special needs so they can be given extra time on exams, such as the SAT, and have an advantage over their peers.

School leaders are given funding by local, state, and federal governments. Usually, this funding is less than what is needed, partly because these sources are wasting money on temporary fixes and ill-conceived programs. Government and private funding sources have decided that traditional university schools of education are failing children and have poured millions, perhaps billions, into alternative certification programs like Teach for America (TFA) and Teaching Fellows.

Yes, this has met teacher shortages, particularly in areas such as special needs instruction, science, and mathematics. But, for the most part, TFA and, to a lesser extent, Teaching Fellows graduates are not committed professionals, and large percentages leave after their two-year commitments, creating a need for even more alternatively certified teachers.

What if these funding sources took this money and gave it to college students who were thinking of entering the teaching profession? The curricula of university schools of education are not perfect. But most college instructors are dedicated professionals committed to training the next generation of teachers. Many are former public educators and others are experts in different instructional areas. Through field experiences, prospective future educators learn from master teachers, an aspect of teacher training absent from alternative certification programs. These future teachers receive support from university clinical supervisors, themselves former teacher trainers, assistant principals, and principals.

How can we build on these traditional programs instead of tossing them aside for costly and dubious alternative programs? First, commit money from funding sources not to alternative programs for people who do not see teaching as their life-long career, but to undergraduate students seriously considering a life-long commitment to teaching.

Bring college freshmen together in the middle of their first year and offer them a program in which they major in a subject area and minor in education so that upon graduation they will become certified teachers. Establish scholarships for those majoring in math or science or other shortage areas if they will commit to *five* years of teaching upon graduation. Have more than a nominal education loan remission program for all graduates who enter and remain in the teaching profession for *10* years.

Universities would need to make program alterations for their students to be eligible for such assistance. They would need to better incorporate fieldwork experiences into instruction and put more stress on practice rather than theory. Student teaching could be expanded to include a full year's internship based on the school district's not the university's calendar. Universities can adapt.

Governments and private supporters are also funding the charter and home-schooling movements. Every public educator should be up in arms against both and not just because they reduce regular education funding or take classroom space from more traditional schools. They are an attack on one of the basic purposes of public education, which is to celebrate the diversity of the population while at the same time insuring that all gain the same basic values that have helped to positively shape America: A work ethic, civic responsibility, tolerance, and respect for the beliefs and cultures of others.

The focus of many (not all) charter schools is narrow, often stressing the superiority of one culture or belief over the importance of accepting all cultures and beliefs. Much home schooling, despite protestations, is an attempt by parents to make sure their children share only the beliefs they wish them to have and to "protect" them from contamination by the ideas and beliefs of others. To paraphrase Oscar Hammerstein, *they have to be taught before it's too late to hate all the beliefs their relatives hate.*

Charter schools, alternative certification programs, No Child Left Behind, scientific testing and measurement of teachers, and increased use of technology have all been touted as panaceas to cure the poor educational system of this country. They are the magic bullets of our generation. There are no panaceas. There are no magic bullets. There are many ways to alleviate the problems in the educational system: End poverty, provide universal health care, provide free parenting workshops, fire incompetent teachers and school leaders, pay master teachers the salaries they deserve, hire school leaders who are themselves master teachers and instructional leaders. We have focused too long on ephemeral cure-alls. Let's, to use an educational phrase, get back to basics.

Another panacea is the movement to have younger school leaders and to appoint those with business rather than educational experience. The last three chancellors of New York City have been business persons, not educators.

Some principals are placed in their positions with only a few years of teaching because of their prior business management experiences.

Education is an art and a profession, not a business. Children are not products from a factory. Having business leaders run schools and school systems is a covert return to a factory model for schools under the guise of scientific measurement and statistics. The leaders of a school, of a district, of a school system should themselves have been master teachers. How can a school leader earn the respect of those he leads and supervises if he has not mastered the art of teaching?

While we have changed the title of those who head schools from "administrators" to "school leaders," we have made them administrators rather than supervisors of teaching and learning to the detriment of the educational system. The principals cited in this book were fortunate to have superintendents who were all former principals and master teachers. They understood the complexities of running a school. But, today many district leaders lack this understanding and look at the school as a corporation rather than as a place of learning.

One cause of this is the reluctance of master teachers to aspire to leadership positions. Some do not want to leave the classroom and the satisfaction of seeing their children learn and grow. Others do not want to deal with the bureaucracy and craziness described in this book. Perhaps, if we could correct some of the issues of school leadership, we would have more master teachers aspiring to be chairs and assistant principals and principals.

Ms. Niles-Perry now teaches leadership courses at her local university. She is often asked by her graduate leadership students, "Do you miss being a principal?" After the account given in this book about the problems she and other principals have faced, her answer may be surprising. She tells her aspiring school leaders:

> Yes, I do often miss it. I miss the thrill—the high, if you will—of having a day where everything just turns out right. A day where even those quick, off-the-cuff decisions work. A day where I helped students, as a group or as individuals, supported teachers, assisted parents and in some small way made my school a better place. All days are exhausting, but such days—and I had many of them—are also invigorating in a way that cannot be duplicated by any other experience. Such days are the equivalent of the runner's high, the grand-slam home run or the touchdown pass. They are the days all principals live and strive for. This is why you want to become school leaders.

Chapter Fourteen

Passing the Baton

Assistant principals advance to become principals. Principals move on to district or university positions. Some leave to take on these new responsibilities. Some decide to retire. A few are retired by the district.

Successful school leaders who have devoted years to their departments and schools do not want the work of their tenures to evaporate as the morning mist when they leave. They can be called successful not because they initiated stunning changes or caused a school to make a great leap forward, but because they leave a legacy that will last long after they are gone, an efficient operation that their successors can build upon. They may have even trained these successors.

The longer school leaders remain in their position, the more they need to add a new priority to their now extensive list: preparing the school or department for their departures. They do this in two important ways. First, they make sure that the systems they put into place will continue to operate after they retire or advance. Second, they train staff members to fill in their positions.

Prior to becoming a principal, Mr. Pfizer was the assistant principal of the math and science department in a Minneapolis middle school. When he began in this position, he found that little was left for him to build upon. The department had been poorly led for several years. Teachers lacked focus. Curricula materials consisted solely of out-of-date state manuals. Test results were below the state and district average.

He worked hard during his eight years as assistant principal. He honed his interpersonal skills to better train his staff and improve the ambience of his department. When he moved up to become a principal, he left a legacy of success in his department that was adopted and then enhanced by his successor. The department he left was far different from the one he inherited:

- School-specific curriculum guides had been created, field tested, revised, and codified for use in all the middle grades. Although teacher teams were credited with these, most of the work was done by Mr. Pfizer.
- Successfully used lesson and unit plans were on file in the department office, available for all to consult and use as needed. New teachers found these invaluable resources.
- Unit examinations, using the format of the state standardized examinations, were created and used in all math and science classes. This insured appropriate coverage of curriculum topics. Students not passing a unit were referred to after-school tutorials so their deficiencies could be remedied. Individual teachers did not have to duplicate efforts creating exams on the same unit. Standardized test results soared.
- The integration of newly hired teachers into the culture of the department and school was a priority. Subject-specific workshops were created and conducted by master teachers. All new teachers were assigned a master teacher "buddy" to help them during their first semester (and second, if needed).
- Through clinical observations, informal conversations, department presentations, and district workshops, Mr. Pfizer honed the skills of his teachers, raising their levels of competency and greatly improving the content and delivery of instruction.
- Mr. Pfizer established a yearly science fair and created math team competitions to highlight the achievement of students and create public venues where children could shine in front of their parents and peers.
- Toward the end of his eight years, Mr. Pfizer, working with a computer savvy teacher in his department, created a math/science website with areas for staff, students, and parents. File materials for teachers were uploaded into the teacher area for easy access. Teachers could post homework assignments, web links, and other materials for students. Parents could check on their children's progress.
- The bulletin boards in math and science rooms were filled with student work and informative and colorful posters related to instruction.
- Science laboratory equipment was upgraded and science labs revamped to make them more motivating, more accessible, and more related to the curriculum. Math classrooms now had class sets of calculators and math manipulatives. Computer stations and Smart Boards had been installed in over half of the math and science classrooms.

Having systems in place is not enough to insure continuity when an assistant principal leaves. When the thought of seeking a principalship first crossed his mind, Mr. Pfizer knew he needed to train a possible successor. He had already seen leadership potential in Ms. Booker, a master teacher with organizational talent and the ability to get along with all members of the school community. He had encouraged her to seek leadership certification and she had enrolled in a program at a local university.

He provided her with leadership experiences. He enlisted her help in training newly assigned teachers. She taught demonstration lessons. She made department presentations on her successful teaching strategies. She became his unofficial assistant, helping with department tasks, from programming to uniform exam preparation, to text ordering, to test scheduling. With the support and help of his principal, he began a campaign to make Ms. Booker "a known quantity." His principal recommended that she help train district teachers and make district presentations. Mr. Pfizer arranged for Ms. Booker to speak at PTA meetings, describing the math and science education programs at the school.

When he left, Mr. Pfizer was confident Ms. Booker could run his department and knew that she would fare well in the selection process as she was well known by parents and the district leaders. After a short stint as the interim acting assistant principal, Ms. Booker was selected to succeed him as math/science chairperson.

On the last day in June, Mr. Pfizer's teachers threw him a party to say goodbye and celebrate his advancement. There were laughter and tears, but his staff knew that even though he would be in another school in another district, their department would continue to function because successful systems were in place and they had confidence in the training he had provided his successor.

Ms. Nguyen, principal of a K–8 Houston elementary school, prepared her school community for her retirement. Fifteen years earlier, she had inherited a well-run school. However, much of its efficiency was based on past practice known to the experienced staff. There was little in writing. Looking at the age of her teachers, she saw that during the next decade over half would retire. She also knew that the average time-commitment of teachers entering the profession was decreasing. The younger generation often sees teaching as a career stop of two or five or ten years, not a lifetime commitment. The days of Mr. Chips are long gone. She combated this using the strategies described in chapters 5, 6, and 7, but knew that higher teacher turnover was a given. She put systems into place.

- With key staff members, she created a *Teacher Handbook*. All school policies were codified. The responsibilities of all administrators and staff members were defined. A newly hired teacher could refer to this handbook to find policies and procedures on everything from grading and promotion to discipline, to fire drills, to parental contacts, to assembly programs, to school trips, etc.
- Likewise, working with staff and parents, she created a *Parent Handbook*. Parents of younger children knew the procedures for the drop-off and pick-up of children. Busing procedures were fully explained. The school's homework policy and discipline code were provided. And the list went on.
- For grades five through eight, a *Student Handbook* was created. Relevant information from the other handbooks was culled and revised to the appropriate level. Important information, such as procedures for moving on to high school, was added.
- Toward the end of her tenure, much of the above was uploaded onto the school's newly created website.
- Ms. Nguyen created a series of weekly bulletins for her staff. As the years passed, these provided a blueprint for the semester, including all the items the staff needed to know at any particular point in the school year. Her successor could use this, along with her weekly desk calendar, to plan for the next school year. During the summer before she moved on to her new position, she added information to her calendar to better assist her successor.

There were many other systems in place, such as her training plan for new teachers. The items mentioned are representative of the paper legacy a principal needs to leave for the next school leader.

Every principal needs an exit strategy. Principals thinking of advancing to district or university positions need to prepare their schools for their departure. Principals planning to retire have a definite time line once they decide on a tentative date. Systems are codified over the full tenure of the principal. Preparing personnel is more time sensitive.

Ms. Niles-Perry faced a unique challenge as she approached retirement. In her large 7–12 Los Angeles school, she had nine assistant principals. Six planned to retire within one year of her own planned retirement. The spasms a school goes through when a principal leaves are bad enough. When an entire leadership team leaves, such tremors become potential cataclysms. Knowing this, she began to prepare personnel three years prior to her projected retirement date.

From the beginning of her principalship, she had encouraged talented teachers to seek supervisory certification. During her final three years, she took this a step further by asking each of her assistant principals to identify possible successors in each of their departments. She considered the three non-retiring assistant principals as possible successors for herself. With the approval of the district, she began to hold after-school supervisory workshops for teachers interested in advancing to leadership positions. As several had leadership certification, she concentrated on the affective and intangible domain of leadership style, introducing and discussing many of her personal strategies.

The concepts were tailored to the culture of her school. After a year of such sessions, some teachers decided to obtain leadership certification. Those already having certification now had the realities of the school to balance the theories of the university. Some decided that they preferred the classroom to the department office, not wanting to give up the satisfaction of working with children for the problems of working with adults. At the end of three years, however, there was a cadre of possible replacements for five of the six department chairs planning to retire. Ms. Niles-Perry had her assistant principal "ducks" lined up.

One of the three assistant principals she considered as her own possible replacement took a principal's position in another school. A second informed her that she too had decided to retire. During her final year Ms. Niles-Perry worked closely with the remaining candidate. All of the systems' pieces were in place. The assistant principal knew these. However, he needed to learn about the personalities of school staff outside his department, of district personnel, of the community board, of the Parent Association, of the newly formed Business Support Team.

There were many conversations and invitations to meetings. Ms. Niles-Perry wanted to be sure this possible successor would enter the position with as much as of her knowledge as possible. The various constituencies mentioned would be represented on the selection committee. Ms. Niles-Perry's work with her potential successor introduced him to these representatives, enhancing his chances for selection to the position. When he was selected, she continued to work with him over her final summer and was on call the next year.

Within two years of her retirement, all those she had trained had moved up to leadership positions in the school, including her own successor. Despite losing almost its entire administrative staff in a short period of time, her school continued to thrive and grow. Students attained higher achievement levels than they had during her administration. Her successor proved more adept than she in gaining financial and other assistance from outside sources. Over time, systems were revisited and revised to adapt to new conditions and regulations.

Every school leader brings new talents to the position. Policies and procedures will change. This is a given. However, new school leaders, no matter how well prepared, need time to acclimate themselves to the culture of a department or school, especially if they come from a different school or district. It is the responsibility of those leaving to make sure systems are in place to allow the school to run efficiently while these new leaders learn their jobs and their schools' cultures. This responsibility is fulfilled even better if those leaving have trained their own replacements from their own schools.

Successful leaders who stretch their tenures longer than they should risk becoming passé and pathetic. We see this in the world of sports when all-star athletes try to stretch their careers for an extra year or two. In 2010, football fans watched as Brett Favre tried to make one more comeback and cringed every time he was sacked or threw yet another interception. Baseball fans of the baby boomer generation remember the final years of Mickey Mantle and Willie Mays when they were shadows of their former selves. As they age, athletes lose that extra step, that split-second timing.

School leaders gain invaluable experience as they mature, but at a certain point the experience gained does not compensate for the quickness of mind lost. This loss of acuity is not physical. The managers of people-oriented organizations feel an accumulation of emotional and psychological stress that wears down their health and personal relationship with their families. Staff, students, and colleagues all want a piece of the school leader every day. The demands of the job lead spouses to believe that the school building is their main rival for the affection of their wives or husbands. As they grow older, children wonder why their mother or father is not there to play and talk with them as much as the parents of their friends.

When does the toll become too much? When will one begin to pay back one's family for years of marriage to the school? When is it time to say goodbye to the job? There is no easy answer.

When Anthony Thelen became AP/Supervision, English and Language Arts, he thought he had the best job in the world. He trained staff, wrote curricula, programmed his department, solved student and parent problems and still taught classes. When there was a conundrum beyond his authority or capability, he sent it upstairs to the principal. Yes, there were some late days and weekends, but not like those of a principal. He still feels the job of assistant principal or chair is the best leadership position for it allows one to use interpersonal and organizational skills while still having the fun and challenge of teaching students.

At a certain point, however, Mr. Thelen saw that his department was running like a well-oiled machine. Sure there were some kinks, like the less-than-satisfactory teacher or the inevitable curricula changes or program snafu, but even these were old hat after nine years. He could stay with this comfortable, but less-than-challenging job or look to the principalship. His wife was supportive, but not enthusiastic. She knew better than he how much being a principal would interfere with their lives.

When the principal of Academic Vocational High School retired, many assistant principals applied for the position, including Mr. Thelen and three of his colleagues in the school. In the 70-year history of the school, every one of its previous five principals had come from within, a silent acknowledgment from the district that the leadership learning curve for the principal of a school with large vocational programs was significant and could be reduced by selecting the next school leader from qualified applicants already onsite.

Mr. Thelen attended training sessions and prep courses to help him with the application and interview process. As he was not sure he wanted to be a principal (and his wife was dubious if she wanted him to be one), he decided to eschew the conventional wisdom and canned answers. He was totally honest in his responses to interview questions. He got the job. For nearly 12 years he devoted himself to the staff and students of Academic Vocational High School. He looks back on those years (and the 10 previous as assistant principal) with great pride.

Now retired for almost 10 years, he reminisces as he looks at a photograph taken at his retirement dinner that included staff members he had trained for leadership positions.

He had hired Hilda, his successor as principal, as an ESL teacher back in the early 1980's when he was still an assistant principal at the school. She later left to become a very successful teacher trainer for the district before returning to the school in the late 1990's to become the assistant principal supervising the social studies department, a department in disarray which she made into a successful team in just one year. During his final year as principal, Mr. Thelen worked with Hilda to help her learn what he knew, for he saw in her a fine successor and the next principal of the high school.

Others in the photo are also his professional children. As principal, he hired and to some extent trained them as teachers during their first year: Ephraim (AP/Mathematics), Nancy (AP/Language Arts), Olivia (AP/Pupil Personnel Services), Daryl (AP/Social Studies and now the next principal), Joe (AP/Administration), Giovanni (AP/Organization), Nina (AP/Art and Fashion Design), Immaculata (Coordinator/Fashion Merchandising). Most of these assistant principals and coordinators attended workshops on becoming a school leader which he offered to members of the school community during his final two years as principal.

Mr. Thelen retired rather young, at age 55. One of the benefits of working for New York City is an excellent pension plan. Simply put, he did not have financial worries and had already lined up a part-time job as a university adjunct. He summed up the reasons for his retirement in his concluding remarks at his farewell dinner:

I would like to end on a lighter note: my top 10 reasons for retiring (with apologies to David Letterman):

10. Good lingual health: I have a reputation for discretion, but it has come at a price. I have bitten my tongue so many times, it's a wonder I can still speak without sounding like Sylvester the cat!
9. I was tired of being a bat. For most of the past 32 years, I left for work at about 6:00 am and returned home after 5 pm. During the middle of winter, daytime was only what I could see from a school window. I was a creature of darkness.
8. Robotics: I began to realize that I was becoming *Star Trek*'s Data. My responses to situations were becoming automatic and programmed. When you become an android, it's time to quit.
7. Sitting through required principals' meetings: My old formula of one cup of coffee for every two hours of meeting was no longer working. My choices were falling asleep in front of the superintendent, becoming addicted to caffeine, or retiring.
6. Breakfast and lunch: Having a leisurely second cup of coffee every morning and a real one-hour break at lunch time. No faxes, no e-mails, no emergencies, no frantic phone calls, no unexpected visitors.

5. The anal-retentive factor: My wife has told me that I've been becoming more anal-retentive each year. To quote a popular expression of my predecessor, Saul, it was time for a high colonic!
4. The narcolepsy factor: I was tired of never really getting a good night's sleep without tossing, mumbling, waking up in a sweat, or seeing yet another course of action at 2 am. Retirement is the best sleeping pill.
3. I wanted to do what I do best: Teach—and the opportunity to do so came along at the right time.
2. I wanted to quit while I was ahead.
1. My LSW: I made a promise to my long suffering wife 12 years ago that I would retire at the earliest possible time. She is much smarter than I. She knew what I didn't: that I'd be married as much to my job as to her. Thank you, my darling, for putting up with me for the past 12 years.

His top ten reasons were quite serious and most school leaders nearing retirement will identify with them.

The most frustrating part of being a school leader is dealing with adults who should know better. There are the parents who blame everyone but themselves for the problems with their children. There are the teachers who are careless with their words and actions and then become indignant when their principal speaks with them about this. There are the assistant principals who feel they can run a school better than their principal and who sometimes think their job is one of power rather than service.

In the end, it comes down to adults who refuse to take responsibility for their own mistakes and shortcomings. This just wears you down, for no matter how much you try to understand and help them, they do not change. It becomes harder and harder for a school leader not to say "How stupid can you be!"

You can also become comfortable with what you've done and reluctant to change. You tend to feel that what worked before will work again. While change for the sake of change must be avoided, becoming resistant to change (as one does as one ages, like it or not), is equally problematic. After 12 years at the helm Mr. Thelen felt that he had taken the school as far as he could with his talents. It was time for someone else, with new ideas and a different set of skills, to take over, initiate needed change, and bring the school to the next level.

Quitting while you're ahead can never be underestimated. The longer you lead a school, the more you realize all the things that can go wrong. An error in judgment, a less-than-thoughtful quick decision, a crisis caused by factors beyond one's control—all could lead to one's dismissal. In today's world past success will not help you. Like teachers, school leaders are disposable. If a school leader is honest, he will admit that as retirement comes closer, he becomes even more careful and conservative, avoiding rocking the boat and seeking to preserve calm. And, the more successful one is, the harder it becomes to do better the next year as the powers that be expect.

All of these items, including one's domestic tranquility, weigh into one's decision to retire. The longer Mr. Thelen served as principal, the more he knew that his wife was right and he should retire as soon as he met the minimum age. He was also confident the next generation was ready to lead the school.

The school leaders described in this book are not charismatic people. They are good managers who established systems—teacher handbooks, student handbooks, procedures for almost every eventuality, etc.—that those who followed them could use during that crucial first year as a school leader and then build upon, revise, or discard as they developed their own leadership style and priorities. They know that if they go back to their schools after they retire, they will find that many of the systems they left are now quite different. This is wonderful, for every school needs to grow with every leader.

Acknowledgments

There is never anything new under the education sun. There is nothing new in this book. Everything in it has been passed down from past generations of teachers and school leaders. It is totally derivative. I can only hope that I have used this collective wisdom in ways informative, enlightening, and even sometimes amusing to you, the reader.

Many people and institutions passed down this lore to me over the span of my career. I could never acknowledge all of them, but there are several to whom I must give credit.

First, a thank you to the principals from whom I learned my trade, Murray Cohn at Louis D. Brandeis High School and Saul Baily at the High School of Fashion Industries. From them, I learned valuable lessons about retaining one's humanity amid the sometimes Kafkaesque world of school and district bureaucracies. I also learned from my many colleagues and fellow principals in the Manhattan High School superintendency. The principalship is a lonely position and one can only really share its burdens with other principals.

Second, thank you to the staffs and students of Brandies High School (1970–1980) and Fashion High (1980–2002). So many there helped me become a good teacher and later a school leader. Special thanks to my talented, dedicated, and supportive team of assistants at Fashion High: Madi, Marcia, Peter, Bill, Nina, Mike, Lorraine, Efraim, Hilda, and Howard—and to Tina, my talented testing coordinator who created the basis for the proctoring instructions mentioned in this text.

Third, thank you to the Manhattan High School superintendents I worked under whose advice and understanding belied the bureaucracy they worked for: Louise, Pat, Steve, Granger, and Tony. Likewise, to the dedicated professionals at the then Board of Education who taught me many of the technical and personal skills needed to lead today's school, among them Larry, John, and Carmen.

Fourth, a thank you to the Fashion Crafts Educational Commission (FCEC), the Liz Claiborne Foundation, and the fashion industry supporters that I worked with over the years, including J. J., Janet, Sal, and Melanie.

Fifth, a profound thank you to Bruce S. Cooper whose encouragement and advice on the world of publishing helped bring this book into existence. And, a thank you to Tom Koerner, Lindsey Schauer, and Melissa McNitt at Rowman & Littlefield Education for advice, help, and assistance.

Finally, a special posthumous thank you to my friend and colleague, Howard Schlesinger, who always helped me remember what was important.

About the Author

Charles A. Bonnici has been an educator for over 40 years, serving as a teacher, assistant principal, and principal in the New York City public school system. Currently, he is an adjunct instructor of educational leadership and Director of School Partnerships for Pace University in New York City. He is the author of *Creating a Leadership Style: Principles of Personal Strategic Planning*, published by Rowman & Littlefield earlier this year.

www.ingramcontent.com/pod-product-compliance
Lightning Source LLC
Chambersburg PA
CBHW021849300426
44115CB00005B/77